An
ESSENTIAL
HISTORY
of
Current
Reading
Practices

Mary Jo Fresch

EDITOR

INTERNATIONAL
Reading Association
800 BARKSDALE ROAD, PO BOX 8139
NEWARK, DE 19714-8139, USA
www.reading.org

To Hank
You are my history

CONTENTS

ABOUT THE EDITOR

MARY JO FRESCH is an associate professor at The Ohio State University at Marion. She teaches literacy and children's literature courses in the School of Teaching and Learning. She began her teaching career as a third-grade teacher in Kent, Ohio. She completed her master's degree in Reading at the University of Akron. She taught at the University of Akron and the University of Nebraska, Lincoln. After completing her doctorate in Reading, Language, and Literature at The Ohio State University, Mary Jo (and family) moved to Melbourne, Australia, where she taught in teacher education programs at the Royal Melbourne Institute of Technology and Deakin University. She joined the faculty at The Ohio State University in 1995. She also directs the Chile study abroad program, a four-week immersion experience for preservice teachers in Concepción, Chile.

Mary Jo's primary research focus is the developmental aspects of becoming a speller and its relationship to teaching and learning. She has published a number of articles, books, and classroom materials related to this research. Her articles have appeared in *The Reading Teacher*, *Reading Online*, *Language Arts*, *Journal of Literacy Research*, and *Reading and Writing Quarterly*. She has coauthored, with Aileen Wheaton, two books (*Teaching and Assessing Spelling* and *The Spelling List and Word Study Resource Book*, Scholastic) and a grades 1 through 6 classroom series (Spelling for Writers, Great Source). Mary Jo has served on a number of International Reading Association committees and Special Interest Group boards.

Mary Jo and her husband, Hank, enjoy many activities together: travel, golf, exercise, and spending time with their children—Angela Thompson (and her husband, Nate) and Michael Fresch (and his fiancée, Lori).

Author Contact Information
Mary Jo can be contacted by e-mail at fresch.1@osu.edu.

CONTRIBUTORS

Patricia A. Alexander
Professor and Distinguished
   Scholar–Teacher
Department of Human
   Development
University of Maryland
College Park, Maryland, USA

Judy Braithwaite
Graduate Level Instructor
Otterbein College
Westerville, Ohio, USA

Michael P. Ford
Professor of Reading Education
University of Wisconsin Oshkosh
Oshkosh, Wisconsin, USA

Emily Fox
Doctoral Student
University of Maryland
College Park, Maryland, USA

Janet H. Hickman
Associate Professor Emerita
The Ohio State University
Columbus, Ohio, USA

Terry Kindervater
K–5 Literacy Specialist
Euclid City Schools
Euclid, Ohio, USA

Sandra McCormick
Professor Emerita
The Ohio State University
Columbus, Ohio, USA

Maureen McLaughlin
Professor of Reading Education
East Stroudsburg University
   of Pennsylvania
East Stroudsburg, Pennsylvania,
   USA

Maryann Mraz
Assistant Professor
Reading and Elementary Education
   Department
University of North Carolina
   at Charlotte
Charlotte, North Carolina, USA

Donna M. Ogle
Professor of Reading and Language
National-Louis University
Chicago, Illinois, USA

Michael F. Opitz
Professor of Reading
University of Northern Colorado
Greeley, Colorado, USA

Nancy Padak
Distinguished Professor
Kent State University
Kent, Ohio, USA

ACKNOWLEDGMENTS

My profound thanks go to the authors of this volume. Thanks for taking time from your busy lives to help create this wonderful work. As educators one and all, we touch the lives of unseen students. You have helped us reach back and learn from those who have provided reading instruction with its rich history. Your work in this volume helps us to reflect on the past and at the same time keeps us moving forward.

Thanks to Corinne Mooney at the International Reading Association for guiding the development of the book. She is a patient professional. Many, many thanks go to Tori Mello Bachman, our developmental editor. Her experience and insights helped shape this volume. Thanks, Tori, for your vision.

I must close with a special acknowledgment to Jerry Zutell. Little did you know, Jerry, when you agreed to be my doctoral advisor nearly 20 years ago that you would become mentor; colleague; and, most important, friend. *Ancora imparo.*

Standing on the Shoulders of Giants

Mary Jo Fresch

This volume provides overviews of essential research and practice for 11 specific areas of reading. These concise chapters written by experts in the field offer a historical perspective on current reading practices and essential readings in each area. Zora Neale Hurston (1942/1996) framed why such a collection is important for educators to consider, stating, "Research is formalized curiosity. It is poking and prying with a purpose. It is a seeking that he who wishes may know the cosmic secrets of the world and that they dwell therein" (p. 143). The chapter authors describe the "poking and prying" that informed, shaped, and gave direction to important areas in the teaching of reading. What "cosmic secrets" were revealed by years of research that inform the theories guiding instruction today? How might we better understand the science of teaching reading?

A full-day institute (Fresch, 2005) at the International Reading Association's 50th Annual Convention inspired this collection. As organizer of the institute I intended to give participants access to eminent scholars whose areas of expertise could enlighten and advance our thinking. Participant response at the end of the day motivated the creation of this collection. Organizing these distinguished educators' insights into a single, edited volume would provide a wider audience with their wisdom. Many of these authors studied under the tutelage of researchers whose work is considered pivotal, many broke ground with their own research, and all offer deep knowledge about their topic.

Gaining Perspective on Change

Putnam (1997) provided a compelling view of why investigation of past research provides perspective for current-day studies:

> If you think reading with phonics is new, it isn't. In 1612 Brinsley...changed the method from learning the sounds of the whole alphabet at once to combining initial consonants with short vowels.... If you think teaching by the sight word method is new, it isn't. Comenius recommended it in 1500.... If you think teaching by the sentence method is new, it isn't. In 1944, I observed a first grade teacher presenting long sentences on oak tag strips.... If you think the tactile-kinesthetic method is new, it isn't. One of the oldest writings in existence is a table of stone, with deep grooves cut for children to move their fingers in or trace.... If you think linguistic methods are new, they are not. Early linguists including Leonard Bloomfield, Henry Lee Smith and Charles Carpenter Fries were recommending teaching by word patterns long ago. (pp. 52–53)

Many of us are surprised by the long histories of these areas of reading. Putnam's challenge to researchers is to do a thorough reading of past studies to inform new research. The researcher's examination of past studies may inform him or her about how to look at data collection in a different way. How might collection of new data extend, enhance, or refute earlier studies? How might a different time and place affect a study? Kliebard (1995) suggested,

> History invites us to reinterpret old questions and sometimes to cast them aside in order to pave the way for new ones. At its best, history provides us with a record of our cumulative experience and suggests how that experience may be interpreted. (p. 198)

Furthermore, reviewing research from a historical perspective reminds us that there are many social, cultural, and political factors influencing education in every era. Venezky's explanation of his view of history reminds the reader that writers interpret these factors as they write. That is, they make decisions about what to include or exclude as significant to their writing. In his *History of Reading Textbooks*, Venezky (1987) stated, "The view of history I espouse is that of multiple causation, that is, that the changes in reader content, instruction technology, and other primary characteristics of education cannot be accounted for by any single factor" (p. 249). Because research does not occur in a vacuum, understanding the external forces of the time may further enlighten researchers. How was the study situated within a particular point in time, paradigm, or controversy? What motivated the researcher in pursuing that study? Insights into these questions can help current-day researchers define their own purposes. The authors of this volume often present multiple factors that led our field to where it is today.

allows us to step back to the point in time when the research was done. Monaghan (1989) maintained that "virtually all academic disciplines incorporate a look at the past into their coursework. The assumption has been that it is intrinsically valuable to know something about those who have trodden a particular path before" (p. 6). We see who we are collectively, as researchers, as well as our role as an individual in that community. How might I contribute to the body of knowledge? What can I learn from the failures and successes of those who have come before me?

Varying Interpretations

The readers of any historical volume must remind themselves that *any* view of history remains in the control of the writer. White (1987) believed "narrative is not merely a neutral discursive form" (p. ix), and Zinn (1994) stated that as writers we can never be strictly neutral. Our personal stance in the type of research we value may influence our selected "lessons to draw on" (Monaghan & Hartman, 2002). And, as White (1987) claimed,

> Certain narrative discourses may have arguments embedded within them, in the form of explanations of why things happened as they did, set forth in the mode of direct address to the reader in the author's own voice and perceivable as such. But such arguments are more properly considered as a commentary on, rather than a part of, the narrative. In historical discourse, the narrative serves to transform into a story a list of historical events that would otherwise be only a chronicle. (p. 43)

The authors in this volume not only share their view of what is important in their areas of expertise, but they also analyze the impact of research and present their interpretations of the important changes 50 years of research bring to the field of education. The challenge, then, is to continue the investigation beyond the histories presented here. These views of the field are, therefore, a jumping-off point for any novice or seasoned researcher. Indeed, researchers will find direction from each author regarding needed research or unanswered questions.

What's Ahead

This volume's authors provide the theories and research they believe best represent current understandings pertaining to their specific topics. As Giroux and Friere noted in the introduction to Shannon's volume (1989), "Theory is always shot through with values and must be seen as both an ethical and political discourse" (p. xi). As well-read scholars, the authors have studied their

In Chapter 1, "Reading in Perspective," Patricia A. Alexander and Emily Fox delineate historic eras of changing attitudes regarding the nature of reading and the role of the reader. Their examination of shifting views about learning provides clarity about influences that have spawned particular methodologies in teaching reading. Alexander and Fox discuss landmark studies and events to help us understand the many debates regarding materials and methods. The authors outline how some historical opposing viewpoints continue as themes in today's research studies. Their chapter is presented first to provide an organizing overview of the nature of reading. The reader will, no doubt, see the foundation laid by Alexander and Fox's chapter in each subsequent chapter.

In Chapter 2, "History of Phonics Instruction," Barbara J. Walker offers a historical look at the teaching of phonics. She provides a personal and scholarly view of the changing landscape of phonics in reading instruction, beginning with her own experiences as a young learner. As many of the authors of this volume do, Walker suggests that the turning point in the history of reading instruction was Flesch's *Why Johnny Can't Read* (1955). Flesch's book provided a political agenda in educating readers. Walker provides the professional, social, and political issues of phonics in the classroom—from teaching with a very strict, skill-and-drill approach to the multiple pathways used today.

"A 50-Year View of Family Literacy" is presented in Chapter 3. Nancy Padak and Terry Kindervater examine the history of research in family literacy. Beginning with Dolores Durkin's 1966 landmark study, *Children Who Read Early*, Padak and Kindervater discuss the various definitions of family literacy. Their chapter provides the research that has demonstrated the important role families play in language development. Federal funding continues to be a deciding factor in the birth and death of various family programs. This chapter provides convincing evidence of the importance educators must place on family literacy and how it can contribute to the development of young learners.

Michael P. Ford and Michael F. Opitz examine the research that has informed and shaped guided reading in Chapter 4, "Guided Reading: Then and Now." Ford and Opitz guide the reader through the years of defining and redefining guided reading. They take us back to the 1940s when Emmett Betts (1946) elaborated on guided reading in his directed reading activity. We are transported through decades of the changing focus on guiding readers in various reading instruction. The authors provide a view of former and current instructional groupings, aims of using guided reading, and current-day

in the teaching of reading but also the changing world of publishing. As a reflection of societal concerns, innovative changes in content and format appeared. Hickman challenges readers to examine their views of literature in reading programs and provides the key research that has demonstrated the value of readers' interactions with such texts. She concludes her chapter with a look toward the digital age. She reminds the reader that whatever form books take in the years to come, we must share with students the joy of reading.

Sandra McCormick and Judy Braithwaite share their observations of the major changes in definitions and approaches for teaching remedial and clinical reading in Chapter 9, "Fifty Years of Remedial and Clinical Reading in the United States: A Historical Overview." Throughout this chapter, the authors indicate that time has helped us eliminate causes we *expected* but later could not verify through research. In fact, the cause-and-effect relationship of reading difficulties took decades to refine and establish with great reliability. While the field has made great strides in understanding struggling readers, there is still much work to be done. McCormick and Braithwaite contextualize the decades with interesting reminders of events such as 32-cent per gallon gasoline, Darth Vader, and the Y2K bug.

Jerry Zutell has titled Chapter 10 "Changing Perspectives on Word Knowledge: Spelling and Vocabulary" because, rather than examining these two areas chronologically, he has organized his topic in a more conceptual manner. In this way, he is able to show us the multiplicity of events that has changed our thinking about how one learns vocabulary and spelling. He examines traditional assumptions and beliefs regarding the teaching and learning of vocabulary and spelling. He then provides the historical studies that have changed our understanding about the nature of the English language (its visual, semantic, and historical patterns), language processes (through Chomsky's investigations), and developmental stages of learning (through Piaget's observations). Zutell provides the studies that have demonstrated the importance of moving students beyond memorization of spelling and vocabulary and into conceptualizing knowledge about the language.

Donna M. Ogle examines "Teacher Education and Professional Development in Reading: 50 Years of Learning" in Chapter 11. Like Zutell, Ogle deals with the array of factors that have made an impact on teacher education. Ogle's conceptual presentation demonstrates the complex issues that have shaped teacher education. A 50-year lens is most appropriate for this chapter, as the beginning studies that examined teacher preparation for reading began in the 1960s. Models such as the Holmes Group are examined, along with the push for

REFERENCES

Adams, M.J. (1990). *Beginning to read: Thinking and learning about print.* Cambridge, MA: MIT Press.

Betts, E.A. (1946). *Foundations of reading instruction.* New York: American Book Company.

Bond, G.L., & Dykstra, R. (1967). The cooperative research program in first-grade reading instruction. *Reading Research Quarterly, 2,* 348–427.

Boote, D.N., & Beile, P. (2005). Scholars before researchers: On the centrality of the dissertation literature review in research preparation. *Educational Researcher, 34,* 3–15.

Chall, J.S. (1967). *Learning to read: The great debate.* New York: McGraw-Hill.

Durkin, D. (1966). *Children who read early.* New York: Teachers College Press.

Flesch, R. (1955). *Why Johnny can't read.* New York: Harper.

Fresch, M.J. (Chair). (2005, May). *The past is prelude to the future: Reflecting over the past 50 years.* Session presented at the annual convention of the International Reading Association, San Antonio, TX.

Hurston, Z.N. (1996). *Dust tracks on a road: An autobiography.* New York: HarperPerennial. (Original work published 1942)

International Reading Association. (n.d.). Writing for *Reading Research Quarterly.* Retrieved July 12, 2005, from www.reading.org/publications/for_authors/rrq.html

Kliebard, H.M. (1995). Why history of education? *Journal of Educational Research, 88,* 194–199.

Monaghan, E.J. (1989). Why study the history of reading? *History of Reading News, 12*(4), 5–6.

Monaghan, E.J., & Hartman, D.K. (2000). Undertaking historical research in literacy. In M.L. Kamil, P.B. Mosenthal, P.D. Pearson, & R. Barr (Eds.), *Handbook of Reading Research* (Vol. 3, pp. 109–121). Mahwah, NJ: Erlbaum.

Moore, D.W., Monaghan, E.J., & Hartman, D.K. (1997). Values of literacy history. *Reading Research Quarterly, 32,* 90–102.

National Council of Teachers of English. (n.d.). Characteristics of publishable manuscripts. Retrieved July 12, 2005, from www.ncte.org/pubs/journals/rte/write/110639.htm

National Institute of Child Health and Human Development. (2000). *Report of the National Reading Panel. Teaching children to read: An evidence-based assessment of the scientific research literature on reading and its implications for reading instruction* (NIH Publication No. 00-4769). Washington, DC: U.S. Government Printing Office.

Otto, W. (1992). The role of research in reading instruction. In S.J. Samuels & A.E. Farstrup (Eds.), *What research has to say about reading instruction* (2nd ed., pp. 1–16). Newark, DE: International Reading Association.

Putnam, L.R. (1997). Beginning reading methods: A review of the past. In W.M. Linek & E.G. Sturtevant (Eds.), *Exploring literacy* (19th yearbook of the College Reading Association, pp. 51–55). Carrollton, GA: College Reading Association.

Shannon, P. (1989). *Broken promises: Reading instruction in twentieth-century America.* Granby, MA: Bergin & Garvey.

Smith, N.B. (2002). *American reading instruction* (Special ed.). Newark, DE: International Reading Association.

Venezky, R.L. (1987). A history of the American reading textbook. *The Elementary School Journal, 87,* 247–265.

White, H.V. (1987). *The content of the form: Narrative discourse and historical representation.* Baltimore: Johns Hopkins University Press.

Zinn, H. (1994). *You can't be neutral on a moving train: A personal history of our times.* Boston: Beacon Press.

A s reading educators face the pressing day-to-day challenges of promoting literacy in schools and in the broader society, they may understandably fail to glance backward at the roots of their field and at the lessons that the rich past has to offer for today's issues and concerns. With this innovative volume, contributors pay tribute to the histories of critical processes and dimensions of reading in the hope of informing the present and foreshadowing the future of reading practice. As with those contributors, we believe that there is a distinct pattern—a particular rhythm—in the development of our understanding of these critical reading processes and dimensions. Further, we hold that while each process or dimension will undoubtedly exhibit its own unique pattern or rhythm in this historical portrayal, each has also been influenced to some degree by the overall shifts and transformations occurring within the field of reading itself. Thus, our goal in this chapter is to provide readers with a more panoramic view of the development of the field of reading research over the last 50 years—a view within which our understanding of specific processes and dimensions of reading might be historically situated.

To frame this historical overview, we describe five eras in reading research and practice that encompass the past 50 years (Alexander & Fox, 2004). These eras are intended to capture views of readers and of the nature of reading prevalent at the time, while still acknowledging alternative perspectives that existed as significant undercurrents of the period. For each era, we discuss critical conditions in reading research and practice, as well as outside the field, that helped to shape that period. Of course, we appreciate that the eras we characterize are approximations of complex, dynamic, and controversial periods in the history of reading and are, therefore, open to debate. Still, we feel that these depictions offer a helpful context within which trends related to individual processes and dimensions can be positioned.

The Era of Conditioned Learning (1950–1965)

Well before the 1950s, reading had been a basic component in school curricula in the United States and had garnered some attention from leading researchers (e.g., Buswell, 1922; Huey, 1908; Thorndike, 1917). Yet, it was not until the post–World War II period that passing flirtations between practitioners and researchers progressed to an established union. Indeed, post–World War II America was fertile ground for significant change in reading. First, there was a spike in births during and immediately following the war leading to a subsequent growth in the school population (Ganley, Lyons, & Sewall, 1993). As the number of school-age children increased, so did the apparent number of

Of course, not all reading researchers or educators of the era bought into this highly deconstructed view of reading or its very linear, sequential mode of controlled instruction. Even some who recognized the relevance of phonics-based approaches as aspects of an instructional program offered more integrated models of reading and called for more balanced approaches to reading pedagogy (Chall, 1967, 1983; Levin, 1965). When problems in reading acquisition persisted and as the drill and practice modes of instruction became perceived as tiresome, dissatisfaction with behavioral solutions grew and the winds of change began to blow.

The Era of Natural Learning (1966–1975)

By the mid-1960s, there was already an apparent unrest with behaviorism as an overarching theory of learning and the "drill and kill" mentality of reading instruction it spawned. Yet, other conditions helped to hasten the fading of the behavioral orientation to reading and the teaching of reading. For one, the 1960s saw the rise of cognitivism as a dominant theory of learning and, consequently, an increased interest in the "black box" of the human mind (Ericsson & Smith, 1991). Researchers were no longer content to focus on behavior. They wanted to understand the thinking behind that behavior (Alexander, 2006).

Certain large-scale projects of the period also proved highly influential, such as the First Grade Studies (Bond & Dykstra, 1967). This federally funded investigation involved the systematic comparison of different approaches to beginning reading instruction by interdisciplinary teams. The influence of two research communities, linguists and psycholinguists, was evident during this era—each with its own twists on the nature of reading and its teaching. For linguists, many following in the tradition of Chomsky (1957, 2002), reading acquisition was linked to an innate capacity for language that was subsequently affected by environmental factors, including instruction. For psycholinguists, the transaction between reader and text was indicative of a natural communicative power best served by a more holistic and aesthetic approach to reading (Goodman & Goodman, 1979; Smith, 1973, 1978). The more naturalistic perspective of both linguists and psycholinguists thus stood in sharp contrast to the "reading-as-conditioned-behavior" perspective of the prior era.

From this perspective, language, like other innate abilities, should be nurtured through meaningful use rather than acquired through mindless repetition. For instance, in his classic volume *Syntactic Structures*, Chomsky (1957) asserted that humans emerge from the womb with a mental template that guides language use. "Languaging" was theorized to unfold naturally following

Even though the linguists, psycholinguists, and sociolinguists shaping the naturalistic era of reading turned our attention inward—away from behavior and into the mind of the reader—there were those who felt this attention to the internal workings of the mind was inadequate or incomplete. These more cognitively oriented researchers were not willing to see reading as quite so natural or to obscure the boundaries between reading, speaking, listening, and writing. The cognitive aspects of reading they emphasized continued to gain momentum and became more definitional for the next era of reading research and practice.

The Era of Information Processing (1976–1985)

By the mid-1970s, at least two converging factors set the stage for yet another theoretical shift in reading research and practice. First, there was the growing attention being paid to the structure and processes of the human mind that had its catalyst in the prior decade (Chi, Glaser, & Farr, 1988; Pearson & Stephens, 1994). The literature on mental structures, problem solving, and expertise was rapidly expanding and coloring research in many psychological and educational fields. At the same time, there was a significant influx in federal funding for basic reading research (Alexander, 1998a). The effect of these converging conditions was the creation of major reading research centers led largely by theorists and researchers whose interests were more in basic than applied research and whose roots were primarily in cognitive psychology (Pearson & Stephens, 1994). The Center for the Study of Reading under Richard Anderson exemplified this trend.

Even though the psycholinguistic undercurrent remained evident during this period, it was cognition, and more specifically information-processing theory, that dominated the reading literature and found its way into reading practice (Anderson, 1977). In effect, the medical metaphor of diagnosis, prescription, and remediation of the 1950s and the learning-as-natural metaphor of the 1960s were replaced with a more mechanistic computer metaphor (Reynolds, Sinatra, & Jetton, 1996). Knowledge, especially prior knowledge, became the focal point of studies trying to understand the interaction between reader and text. Learning was presumed to occur when information from the environment (text) became part of an individual's knowledge base—a process that involved the input, interpretation, organization, retention, and output of information (Samuels & Kamil, 1984).

The body of research on knowledge spawned by this era remains one of its enduring legacies (Alexander, 1998a; Alexander & Murphy, 1998). Readers' rival view was an increased concern for the aesthetic of reading (Rosenblatt, 1978/1994) and a rather negative attitude toward knowledge as the residue of information-getting or fact-finding (Rosenblatt, 1978/1994, p. 23). This unfavorable view of knowledge as information-getting was well represented in the writings of Louise Rosenblatt (1978/1994), especially her classic treatise *The Reader, the Text, the Poem: The Transactional Theory of the Literary Work*. From this perspective, the goal was to lose oneself *in* the text and not specifically to learn *from* it (see also Chapter 5, this volume, for further discussion of Rosenblatt's works).

The Era of Sociocultural Learning (1986–1995)

By the mid-1980s, the mechanistic computer metaphor that guided information-processing research was losing its appeal (Anderson, Reder, & Simon, 1996) and was soon replaced by a constructivist orientation that gave individuals a more active role in their learning (Reynolds et al., 1996). The interventions built around information-processing theory also failed to fulfill their earlier promise, as too many students continued to struggle to learn from text (Harris, 1996). Another force for change that appeared on the horizon was the rising popularity of writings in social and cultural anthropology, especially the works of Vygotsky (1962/1986), Lave (1988), and others (e.g., Heath, 1983; Rogoff, 1990). These writings sparked increased acceptance of ethnographic and qualitative modes of inquiry, along with studies of literacy practices involving naturally occurring texts read in natural settings, such as classrooms, homes, and workplaces (Anderson, Wilson, & Fielding, 1988). To reflect this more holistic, integrated view, the journal of the National Reading Conference, *Journal of Reading Behavior*, was retitled the *Journal of Literacy Research* in 1996.

Another catalyst for change during this time was a mounting distrust or devaluing of formal, individual knowledge (Sfard, 1998). It was the process of learning rather than its products that appeared to matter most. Even though *knowledge* was still a frequently used term in literacy research and practice, it took on a new character. For one, knowledge now encompassed an array of diverse forms and interactive dimensions that had to be coordinated or reconciled in the performance of any nontrivial literacy act (Alexander, Schallert, & Hare, 1991; Paris, Lipson, & Wixson, 1983; Prawat, 1989).

There was also a growing awareness that knowledge was not always a positive force in students' learning and development. An individual's or group's inaccurate or inadequately grounded knowledge could impede or interfere with future learning (Chinn & Brewer, 1993; Perkins & Simmons, 1988). Research

the aesthetic response to literature (Oldfather & Wigfield, 1996). However, in the late 1990s, the rich and impressive body of motivation research migrated into the reading community (Guthrie & Wigfield, 2000) and led to the consideration of such factors as learners' interest, goals, and active participation in text-based learning (Almasi, McKeown, & Beck, 1996; Hidi, 1990; Schallert, Meyer, & Fowler, 1995; Turner, 1995). The result of this infusion was a reconceptualization of the student as engaged or motivated reader (Guthrie & Wigfield, 2000).

Finally, it has become increasingly more difficult for researchers and practitioners to ignore that reading relates not only to the young or struggling reader, the focus of most prior research, but also to readers of all abilities and ages. That is, reading development extends beyond the initial phase of acquisition to encompass a reader's lifelong engagement in a range of reading-related, goal-directed activities (Alexander, 2006). The current initiatives directed toward adolescent and adult readers are reflective of this developmental orientation (National Institute of Child Health and Human Development, 2000; RAND Reading Study Group, 2002). Also indicative of this reframing was the recognition that earlier dichotomization of reading into "learning to read" and "reading to learn" stages (Chall, 1983, p. 20) missed the inherent relation between learning *in* reading and learning *with* reading.

Applying a label to an ongoing era is certainly a risky venture. However, the label *engaged* captures the aforementioned forces shaping perceptions of reading research and practice. For instance, engagement portrays readers as active and willful participants in their learning, rather than as passive receptacles of information (Guthrie & Wigfield, 2000; Reed & Schallert, 1993; Reed, Schallert, & Goetz, 1993). This portrait of the engaged reader has both individualistic and collective dimensions; it attends not only to the motivations and knowledge of the individual but also to their interactions with others inside and outside the classroom (Guthrie, McGough, Bennett, & Rice, 1996; Guthrie, Van Meter, et al., 1996). Finally, from this vantage point, students are not yet fully developed as readers when they can master basic linguistic skills. Rather, they continue to grow in their linguistic knowledge, subject-matter knowledge, strategic capabilities, and motivations throughout their lifetimes (Alexander, 1997).

Despite this strong orientation toward engagement, a rival perspective on reading exists and appears to be growing in strength as we proceed into the 21st century. We label this rival perspective as *reconditioning* to signal certain features of this undercurrent. First, as with behaviorism, this rival stance pertains to the identification, teaching, and remediation of the reading subskills or components underlying reading acquisition (e.g., Foorman, Francis, Fletcher,

community is proactive or reactive in relation to such powerful external forces.

3. Certain fundamental issues occur and reoccur across the history of reading research and practice. As with education more broadly, there are iterative trends that have marked the past 50 years of reading research (Alexander, Murphy, & Woods, 1996). The correlated appearance of these trends has served to give each era its distinct character. For reading, those iterative trends include the shifting emphasis on whole-word or phonetic instructional approaches, as well as the variable concern for the individual mind or for the social group. Other recurring themes include the use of controlled or highly structured materials or more authentic, naturally occurring texts (Rosenblatt, 1978/1994) and a rising or falling concern for subject-matter knowledge (Alexander, 1998a). There is every possibility that these same trends will be evident in the future eras of reading research and practice. At a minimum, the iterative nature of reading research trends reminds us that many current initiatives have roots that reach deep into the history of our investigations of reading.

4. The eras of reading research reveal a changing emphasis on physiological, psychological, and social variables. Reading always involves physiological, psychological, and sociological forces. Yet each era puts differential weight on those forces. For example, physiology, which focuses on the biological, chemical, and neurological dimensions of human performance, was strongly influential during the conditioning era and is beginning to reemerge as part of the reconditioning movement we now see in reading research and practice. By comparison, psychological orientations that pertain to the mind and mental processes were quite apparent in the era of information processing. Finally, there have been periods in reading research and practice when the focus has been on human-to-human interactions and on group processes. The current engagement era places a great deal of emphasis on such social aspects of learning. At present, improvements in technologies that allow researchers to look deeper into the structure and processes of the mind (e.g., fMRIs) may give greater impetus to physiological aspects of reading than in eras past. Similarly, the expanding presence of hypermedia in the lives of students suggests a future era in which the social and psychological dimensions of hypermedia learning and teaching gain prominence.

5. The cycle of changes observed in the history of reading research suggests developmental maturation of the field. In the movement from era to era portrayed here, we see a field that is becoming progressively more sophisticated and inclusive. Researchers in each succeeding generation have investigated a wider and more complex range of phenomena. This changing pattern is partly

unpleasant or even detrimental effects on the very readers these innovations are presumed to help.

Recommendation 2: *Become a bit of a reading historian.* We appreciate that time is a prized commodity for reading educators. However, we would hope that some time can be set aside to glance back toward reading's past in search of insights into today's problems or concerns. Our list of essential readings includes a number of classic chapters and articles that provide a good foundation for understanding the history of reading education and research. Certainly, having a volume like this one is a great aid in exploring the progress made across a range of reading processes or features. Fortunately, in this hypermedia age, it is quite easier to search for a particular topic or question on the Internet as well.

Recommendation 3: *Take a global look at specific issues.* At the outset of this chapter, we discussed reading's history as a confluence of events and factors. We believe that this same principle applies to the instruction that unfolds in one classroom for one teacher over time. As practitioners, we must keep in mind that effective reading instruction cannot be isolated to one variable (e.g., fluency, comprehension, or phonemic awareness) practiced via one approach (e.g., cooperative learning or book clubs) with any one group (e.g., struggling readers or learners with limited English proficiency). Effective instruction, like the history of reading, is best understood as the confluence of all of these elements at any one moment in our classrooms as well as over the course of our professional careers.

Final Thoughts

> The moments of the past do not remain still; they retain in our memory the motion which drew them towards the future, towards a future which has itself become the past, and draw us on in their train. (Proust, 1925/1930, p. 100)

What is it about the topic of reading's history that made this such an intriguing realm of inquiry for us, as authors? Upon reflection, we can identify at least four reasons that compel us to look backward at the decades and centuries past, not only for this volume but also in our prior writings (Alexander & Fox, 2004). First, we have had the benefit of living through many of the eras we describe in these pages, and firsthand experience can be a powerful teacher if we allow it to be. Second, we believe strongly that change is not random but can be understood as a confluence of factors and events that arise over time—a confluence that results in discernible trends with discernible effects. We have been captivated with trying to unearth and plot those trends both in the domain of

Kamil, P.B. Mosenthal, P.D. Pearson, & R. Barr (Eds.), *Handbook of reading research* (Vol. 3, pp. 53–74). Mahwah, NJ: Erlbaum.

Kamil, M.L. (1984). Current traditions of reading research. In P.D. Pearson, R. Barr, M.L. Kamil, & P. Mosenthal (Eds.), *Handbook of reading research* (pp. 39–62). New York: Longman.

Pearson, P.D., & Stephens, D. (1994). Learning from literacy: A 30-year journey. In R.B. Ruddell, M.R. Ruddell, & H. Singer (Eds.), *Theoretical models and processes of reading* (4th ed., pp. 22–42). Newark, DE: International Reading Association.

Venezky, R.L. (1984). The history of reading research. In P.D. Pearson, R. Barr, M.L. Kamil, & P. Mosenthal (Eds.), *Handbook of reading research* (pp. 3–38). New York: Longman.

REFERENCES

Afflerbach, P., & VanSledright, B. (2001). Hath! Doth! What? Middle graders reading innovative history text. *Journal of Adolescent & Adult Literacy, 44,* 696–707.

Alexander, P.A. (1997). Mapping the multidimensional nature of domain learning: The interplay of cognitive, motivational, and strategic forces. In M.L. Maehr & P.R. Pintrich (Eds.), *Advances in motivation and achievement* (Vol. 10, pp. 213–250). London: JAI Press.

Alexander, P.A. (1998a). Knowledge and literacy: A transgenerational perspective. In T. Shanahan & F.V. Rodriguez-Brown (Eds.), *47th yearbook of the National Reading Conference* (pp. 22–43). Chicago: National Reading Conference.

Alexander, P.A. (1998b). The nature of disciplinary and domain learning: The knowledge, interest, and strategic dimensions of learning from subject-matter text. In C. Hynd (Ed.), *Learning from text across conceptual domains* (pp. 263–287). Mahwah, NJ: Erlbaum.

Alexander, P.A. (2006). The path to competence: A lifespan developmental perspective on reading. *Journal of Literacy Research, 37,* 413–436.

Alexander, P.A., & Fox, E. (2004). A historical perspective on reading research and practice. In R.B. Ruddell & N.J. Unrau (Eds.), *Theoretical models and processes of reading* (5th ed., pp. 33–68). Newark, DE: International Reading Association.

Alexander, P.A., & Jetton, T.L. (2003). Learning from traditional and alternative texts: New conceptualizations for the information age. In A.C. Graesser, M.A. Gernsbacher, & S.R. Goldman (Eds.), *Handbook of discourse processes* (pp. 199–241). Mahwah, NJ: Erlbaum.

Alexander, P.A., & Judy, J.E. (1988). The interaction of domain-specific and strategic knowledge in academic performance. *Review of Educational Research, 58,* 375–404.

Alexander, P.A., & Knight, S.L. (1993). Dimensions of the interplay between learning and teaching. *Educational Forum, 57,* 232–245.

Alexander, P.A., & Murphy, P.K. (1998). The research base for APA's learner-centered principles. In N.M. Lambert & B.L. McCombs (Eds.), *Issues in school reform: A sampler of psychological perspectives on learner-centered schools* (pp. 25–60). Washington, DC: American Psychological Association.

Alexander, P.A., Murphy, P.K., Buehl, M.M., & Sperl, C.T. (1997, December). *The influence of prior knowledge, beliefs, and interest in learning from persuasive text.* Paper presented at the annual meeting of the National Reading Conference, Scottsdale, AZ.

Alexander, P.A., Murphy, P.K., & Woods, B.S. (1996). Of squalls and fathoms: Navigating the seas of educational innovation. *Educational Researcher, 25*(3), 31–36, 39.

Alexander, P.A., Schallert, D.L., & Hare, V.C. (1991). Coming to terms: How researchers in

Resnick (Ed.), *Knowing, learning, and instruction: Essays in honor of Robert Glaser* (pp. 453–494). Hillsdale, NJ: Erlbaum.

Duffy, G., Roehler, L.R., Meloth, M.S., & Vavrus, L.G. (1986). Conceptualizing instructional explanation. *Teaching and Teacher Education, 2,* 197–214.

Ericsson, K.A., & Smith, J. (1991). *Toward a general theory of expertise: Prospects and limits.* New York: Cambridge University Press.

Flesch, R. (1955). *Why Johnny can't read.* New York: Harper & Brothers.

Foorman, B.R., Francis, D.J., Fletcher, J.M., Schatschneider, C., & Mehta, P. (1998). The role of instruction in learning to read: Preventing reading failure in at-risk children. *Journal of Educational Psychology, 90,* 37–55.

Ganley, A.C., Lyons, T.T., & Sewall, G.T. (1993). *The U.S.A. since 1945: After Hiroshima* (3rd ed.). White Plains, NY: Longman.

Gardner, H. (1991). *The unschooled mind: How children think and how schools should teach.* New York: Basic Books.

Garner, R. (1987). *Metacognition and reading comprehension.* Norwood, NJ: Ablex.

Garner, R., & Hansis, R. (1994). Literacy practices outside of school: Adults' beliefs and their responses to "street texts." In R. Garner & P.A. Alexander (Eds.), *Beliefs about text and instruction with text* (pp. 57–73). Hillsdale, NJ: Erlbaum.

Glaser, R. (1978). The contributions of B.F. Skinner to education and some counterinfluences. In P. Suppes (Ed.), *Impact of research on education: Some case studies* (pp. 199–265). Washington, DC: National Academy of Education.

Goetz, E.T., Alexander, P.A., & Ash, M.J. (1992). *Educational psychology: A classroom perspective.* Columbus, OH: Merrill.

Goodman, K.S. (1965). A linguistic study of cues and miscues in reading. *Elementary English, 42,* 639–643.

Goodman, K.S., & Goodman, Y.M. (1979). Learning to read is natural. In L.B. Resnick & P.A. Weaver (Eds.), *Theory and practice in early reading* (pp. 137–154). Hillsdale, NJ: Erlbaum.

Greeno, J.G., & Moore, J.L. (1993). Situativity and symbols: Response to Vera and Simon. *Cognitive Science, 17,* 49–59.

Guthrie, J.T., McGough, K., Bennett, L., & Rice, M.E. (1996). Concept-oriented reading instruction: An integrated curriculum to develop motivations and strategies for reading. In L. Baker, P. Afflerbach, & D. Reinking (Eds.), *Developing engaged readers in school and home communities* (pp. 165–190). Hillsdale, NJ: Erlbaum.

Guthrie, J.T., Van Meter, P., McCann, A., Wigfield, A., Bennett, L., Poundstone, C., et al. (1996). Growth of literacy engagement: Changes in motivations and strategies during concept-oriented reading instruction. *Reading Research Quarterly, 31,* 306–332.

Guthrie, J.T., & Wigfield, A. (2000). Engagement and motivation in reading. In M.L. Kamil, P.B. Mosenthal, P.D. Pearson, & R. Barr (Eds.), *Handbook of reading research* (Vol. 3, pp. 403–422). Mahwah, NJ: Erlbaum.

Halliday, M.A.K. (1969). Relevant models of language. *Educational Review, 22,* 26–37.

Halliday, M.A.K., & Hasan, R. (1976). *Cohesion in English.* New York: Longman.

Hansen, J. (1981). The effects of inference training and practice on young children's reading comprehension. *Reading Research Quarterly, 16,* 391–417.

Harris, K.R. (1996, April). *The state of strategy research: Is this old territory or are there new frontiers?* Panel discussion presented at the annual meeting of the American Educational Research Association, New York.

Harste, J.C., Burke, C., & Woodward, V.A. (1984). *Language stories and literacy lessons.* Portsmouth, NH: Heinemann.

Heath, S.B. (1982). What no bedtime story means: Narrative skills at home and school. *Language in Society, 11,* 49–76.

Heath, S.B. (1983). *Ways with words: Language, life, and work in communities and classrooms.* New York: Cambridge University Press.

Hidi, S. (1990). Interest and its contribution as a mental resource for learning. *Review of Educational Research, 60,* 549–571.

Huey, E.B. (1908). *The psychology and pedagogy of reading.* New York: Macmillan.

Kintsch, W., & van Dijk, T.A. (1978). Toward a model of text comprehension and production. *Psychological Review, 85,* 363–394.

Labov, W. (1966). *The social stratification of English in New York City.* Washington, DC: Center for Applied Linguistics.

Labov, W. (1971). Systematically misleading data from test questions. *Urban Review, 9*(3), 146–170.

Labov, W. (1972). *Sociolinguistic patterns.* Philadelphia: University of Pennsylvania Press.

Lave, J. (1988). *Cognition and practice.* Cambridge, England: Cambridge University Press.

Levin, H. (Ed.). (1965). *Planning for a reading research program.* Ithaca, NY: Cornell University.

academic discourse tasks. Paper presented at the annual meeting of the American Educational Research Association, Atlanta, GA.

Resnick, L.B., Levine, J.M., & Teasley, S.D. (1991). *Perspectives on socially shared cognition*. Washington, DC: American Psychological Association.

Reynolds, R.E., Sinatra, G.M., & Jetton, T.L. (1996). Views of knowledge acquisition and representation: A continuum from experience centered to mind centered. *Educational Psychologist, 31*, 93–104.

Rogoff, B. (1990). *Apprenticeship in thinking: Cognitive development in social context*. New York: Oxford University Press.

Rosenblatt, L. (1994). *The reader, the text, the poem: The transactional theory of the literary work*. Carbondale: Southern Illinois University Press. (Original work published 1978)

Ruddell, R.B. (2002). *Teaching children to read and write: Becoming an effective literacy teacher* (3rd ed.). Boston: Allyn & Bacon.

Rumelhart, D.E. (1980). Schemata: The building blocks of cognition. In R.J. Spiro, B.C. Bruce, & W.F. Brewer (Eds.), *Theoretical issues in reading comprehension: Perspectives from cognitive psychology, linguistics, artificial intelligence, and education* (pp. 33–58). Hillsdale, NJ: Erlbaum.

Salomon, G. (1993). *Distributed cognitions: Psychological and educational considerations*. Cambridge, England: Cambridge University Press.

Samuels, S.J., & Kamil, M.L. (1984). Models of the reading process. In P.D. Pearson, R. Barr, M.L. Kamil, & P. Mosenthal (Eds.), *Handbook of reading research* (pp. 185–224). New York: Longman.

Schallert, D.L., Meyer, D.K., & Fowler, L.A. (1995). The nature of engagement when reading in and out of one's discipline. In K.A. Hinchman, D.J. Leu, & C.K. Kinzer (Eds.), *Perspectives on literacy research and practice* (44th yearbook of the National Reading Conference, pp. 119–125). Chicago: National Reading Conference.

Sfard, A. (1998). On two metaphors for learning and the dangers of choosing just one. *Educational Researcher, 27*(2), 4–13.

Shaywitz, B.A., Fletcher, J.M., Holahan, J.M., & Shaywitz, S.E. (1992). Discrepancy compared to low achievement definitions of reading disability: Results from the Connecticut Longitudinal Study. *Journal of Learning Disabilities, 25*, 639–648.

Shuy, R.W. (1968). Detroit speech: Careless, awkward, and inconsistent, or systematic, graceful, and regular? *Elementary English, 45*, 565–569.

Shuy, R.W. (1969). Some considerations for developing beginning reading materials for ghetto children. *Journal of Reading Behavior, 1*, 33–43.

Smith, C.E., & Keogh, B.K. (1962). The group Bender-Gestalt as a reading readiness screening instrument. *Perceptual and Motor Skills, 15*, 639–645.

Smith, F. (1973). *Psycholinguistics and reading*. Austin, TX: Holt, Rinehart and Winston.

Smith, F. (1978). *Understanding reading: A psycholinguistic analysis of reading and learning to read* (2nd ed.). Austin, TX: Holt, Rinehart and Winston.

Smith, F. (1985). A metaphor for literacy: Creating worlds or shunting information? In D.R. Olson, N. Torrance, & A. Hildyard (Eds.), *Literacy, language, and learning: The nature and consequences of reading and writing* (pp. 1–39). Hillsdale, NJ: Erlbaum.

Snyder, R.T., & Freud, S.L. (1967). Reading readiness and its relation to maturational unreadiness as measured by the spiral aftereffect and other visual-perceptual techniques. *Perceptual and Motor Skills, 25*, 841–854.

Spiro, R.J., & Jehng, J.C. (1990). Cognitive flexibility and hypertext: Theory and technology for the nonlinear and multidimensional traversal of complex subject matter. In D. Nix & R.J. Spiro (Eds.), *Cognition, education, and multimedia: Exploring ideas in high technology* (pp. 163–205). Hillsdale, NJ: Erlbaum.

Spivey, N.N., & King, J.R. (1989). Readers as writers composing from sources. *Reading Research Quarterly, 24*, 7–26.

Thorndike, E.L. (1917). Reading as reasoning: A study of mistakes in paragraph reading. *Journal of Educational Psychology, 8*, 323–332.

Tierney, R.J., Readence, J.E., & Dishner, E.K. (1990). *Reading strategies and practices: A compendium* (3rd ed.). Boston: Allyn & Bacon.

Tierney, R.J., Soter, A., O'Flahavan, J.F., & McGinley, W. (1989). The effects of reading and writing upon thinking critically. *Reading Research Quarterly, 24*, 134–173.

Torgesen, J.K. (1998). Instructional interventions for children with reading disabilities. In B.K. Shapiro, P.J. Accardo, & A.J. Capute (Eds.), *Specific reading disability: A view of the spectrum* (pp. 197–200). Timonium, MD: York Press.

Torgesen, J.K. (1999). Reading disabilities. In R. Gallimore, L. Bernheimer, D.L. MacMillan, D. Speece, & S. Vaughn (Eds.), *Developmental perspectives on children with high incidence*

CHAPTER 2

History of Phonics Instruction

Barbara J. Walker

Barbara J. Walker

It was the early 1950s, and I slowly walked to my first school experience wondering what lay ahead in first grade. Public schools weren't really ready for the baby boomers. Large numbers of students in the classrooms made the easygoing curriculum of the past obsolete. For instance, there were 24 other students in my first-grade classroom. As all first-grade teachers did, Mrs. Railsback introduced us to Dick, Jane, and Sally basic readers. We had big charts of Dick and Jane in the front of the room where we could match the picture of Dick with his name. I can still remember the day we saw the picture of Spot, their dog. My dad really wanted a dog, so learning that word was important to me.

In the 1950s, teachers used the whole-word reading method, where they introduced the printed word along with a picture and then used the word in a meaningful sentence. We had to listen closely to what the teacher was saying and then look closely at the whole word and its form as we looked at a large chart. In second grade, the situation worsened. I had to do phonics workbook pages. What a nightmare! I could not then—and still cannot—synthesize sounds (blend the separate sounds to form a word). Therefore, phonics in isolation was difficult for me. However, synthesizing letter sounds is not the only way to figure out words. I used meaning, my experiences, and the pictures to figure out words.

An Essential History of Current Reading Practices, edited by Mary Jo Fresch.
© 2008 by the International Reading Association.

meaningful reading, usually appearing in the second and third grades. Teachers were admonished to not "reinstate the old mechanical phonic drills," which would result in word-by-word reading (Gray, 1948, p. 28). During the 1950s, most reading professionals believed that if a student could recognize a large number of words instantly, he or she could use the sentence context to read unfamiliar words.

To learn words, children needed many repetitions before unfamiliar words became part of their sight word vocabulary. Through multiple repetitions of words, children would learn to read printed words and use context to promote learning new words. The basic readers, forerunner of the basal readers, included a lot of repetition, using phrases similar to the following:

See Max, said Jane.

See Max run.

Run, Max, run.

In fact, looking at whole words and repeating them frequently does work when children have to know only a small number of words.

Even though the reading program promoted word perception, Gray (1960) claimed that children needed other strategies, too. He suggested that as children read unfamiliar words, other clues might help readers. He suggested four major ways to aid word perception: "1) memory of word form, 2) context clues, 3) word analysis (structural and phonetic), and 4) the dictionary" (p. 16). He did include phonetic clues, but they were low on his list of what to use when encountering an unfamiliar word. The prevalent view was that basic readers provided enough repetitions so that children would learn to recognize words naturally. Dick, Jane, and Sally and their precursors would set the standard for reading instruction from the 1930s through the 1960s.

During the latter part of the 1950s, there was a growing concern that no strategies for analyzing unfamiliar words were being taught. Parents were getting anxious wanting their children to learn and use phonic knowledge. In 1955, when Rudolf Flesch published *Why Johnny Can't Read*, phonics instruction gained credibility. Flesch (1955) maintained children hesitated when they came to an unknown word. He advocated that children should learn to sound out words so they could recognize unknown words readily. The book sold over a half-million copies (see also chapters 1, 5, 7, and 9, this volume, for more discussion of Flesch's work). Parents and the public read the book and began to advocate for more phonics instruction. However, publishers

readers contained very stilted language using words with the same graphic ending as the recurrent written pattern of /an/ in *man*, *ran*, and *fan*. Teachers introduced the words in a list. For example, a story using both the /at/ and /an/ patterns would read as the following:

A fat man ran.

Fan the fat man.

Dan ran to the fat man.

Dan can fan the fat man.

Other programs taught sound–symbol relationships at the onset of schooling. Following the thinking of the behaviorists, teachers introduced rules like short "a" and then the children read stories that had short "a" words.

The late 1960s was a time of great controversy. We, the children who learned to read with Dick, Jane, and Sally, were demanding change. We had learned that in the real world not all families were like Dick, Jane, and Sally. We wanted that changed! Therefore, some of us worked toward civil rights for all races; others demonstrated against the war; still others worked for more innovative views of learning and education. Learning to read also had its growing controversies. Several groups of professionals developed very different lines of thinking. Skinner (1958, 1965) developed the science of human behavior, or behaviorism, which viewed learning as a stimulus–response interaction (see also chapters 1 and 9, this volume, for further discussion of behaviorism). This view supported synthetic phonics instruction (sounding out words letter by letter) and the skills movement (teaching discrete parts of reading). The work of Gibson (1964, 1965) on word perception studied what students focused on when reading whole words. This research also supported the idea that there were subabilities, such as visual memory, that underlie reading; therefore, researchers continued the search for underlying aspects of reading. Holmes (1965) was working on the substrata theory of reading, which would identify other attributes that might underlie reading. Chomsky (1965) hypothesized that children were "wired" or biologically predisposed to acquire basic syntax or grammatical structures (see also chapters 1, 5, and 10, this volume, for further discussion of Chomsky's work). Even young children could produce an infinite number of novel sentences. Building on the syntax perspective, Goodman (1967) wrote the seminal piece "Reading: A Psycholinguistic Guessing Game." Other research in linguistics, psycholinguistics, and sociolinguistics segued into literacy instruction and later had a profound effect on beginning reading

Phonics: Anything Goes

Where should one begin when talking about phonics instruction in the 1970s? Due to the First Grade Studies and *Learning to Read: The Great Debate*, it appeared that many different approaches were acceptable, as long as teachers used some type of phonics instruction. The previous decade demonstrated that phonics instruction, whether it was intensive or gradual, improves students' word learning. Project Literacy occurred at the same time and focused on word perception and perceptual development. However, Gibson and the research team found that readers used distinctive features of word units rather than word configuration or recognizing the whole word (Gibson, 1965; Gibson & Levin, 1975). This marked the end of only teaching whole words. Additionally, Gibson along with her colleagues investigated the nature of the correspondence between written and spoken language; they found that invariable units (sound–symbol patterns) resulted in better perception for reading words (Gibson, Pick, Osser, & Hammond, 1962). The public believed the research endorsed all sound–symbol relationships. This misreading of Gibson's findings indirectly "endorsed decoding instruction" (Williams, 1984, p. 14). Taken together, these findings resulted in a plethora of basal reading programs in the early 1970s. The various basal reading companies worked to include more phonics instruction earlier; as a result, some publishers started analytic phonics instruction during kindergarten. For phonics instruction as well as reading processes, the research continued. Some researchers focused on the active role of the reader in the developing field of cognitive psychology, the study of how learners actively "build" knowledge.

However, the behaviorist viewpoint dominated instruction in the 1970s. The work of behavioral psychologists had a growing influence on reading instruction during this decade. Gagne (1970) purported that task analysis was important for learning complex tasks such as reading. The behaviorist view broke reading into its component skills; each skill had a determined sequence of subskills (discrete, small tasks of reading). Many educators and basal reading publishers jumped on this bandwagon. They dissected phonics instruction into minute subskills and sequenced them for reading instruction. Teachers taught certain consonants first, second, and so forth. The most interesting debate in classrooms was whether you taught the short "a" along with the long "a" or taught all the short vowel sounds first, then the long vowel sounds. Some reading professionals were convinced that an accumulation of subskills would produce a reader. Teachers used separate phonics workbooks in tandem with basal readers. Skills programs such as *Sullivan Programmed Readers*, in which

Of these programs, Distar reading (currently known as Reading Mastery) consistently produced significant growth in word recognition (Bereiter & Engelmann, 1970). Distar introduced sounds slowly and demonstrated how to blend sounds. This improved phonemic synthesis (blending sounds). The program also used hand signals to direct attention to letters as students sounded out the words. Students spent a great deal of time learning to sound out words and then saying them fast. Teachers introduced stories later in the program. In spite of learning to blend sounds, the slow pace for learning words and reading stories, this program did not match how average students learned. Average students learn sound–symbol relationships more readily and move to longer stories much sooner.

The sequences of hierarchal skill development, as well as the systematic blending of sounds, were intrusive ways to develop phonic knowledge. Little actual reading occurred in classrooms because of the concentrated focus on skill instruction in phonics and the subsequent testing of phonic knowledge. This approach certainly had its opponents. Some believed that code instruction (learning letters and their sounds) had no place in a reading program.

Teachers using the Language Experience Approach, one of the methods used in the First Grade Studies, did not believe in direct instruction in letter–sound relationships. In this approach, children dictated a story and the teacher used the story to teach the children to read. A collection of the stories was the child's first reader. From the dictated language experience stories, the teacher selected initial consonants and simple vowel combinations to develop phonic knowledge. During the 1970s, with the work of Stauffer (1970) and Van Allen (1976), language experience gathered supporters for teaching reading this way.

The emerging cognitive revolution led to an increased focus on constructing meaning using readers' prior knowledge and text knowledge simultaneously (Pearson & Stephens, 1994). Reading research shifted away from word learning and focused on meaning. Comprehension and constructing meaning were the foci of the federally funded research in the 1980s. At the same time, the concept of constructing meaning became the core of the whole-language movement. Thus, the whole-language movement would hold court against the skills approach and continue to grow throughout the 1980s and 1990s.

Phonics Drill Dies a Slow Death

During the 1980s, phonics-first programs and skill instruction decreased in use and basal readers included more literature-based stories because of the growing influence of whole language. In the mid-1980s, Anderson and his colleagues

cues); using the letters and their sounds (graphophonic cues), and the grammar of the sentence (syntactic cues). The teachers asked if what the student read made sense (semantic cue), asked what would make sense and start with the sound of the beginning letter (graphophonic cue), or asked if how the student read the sentence sounded like spoken English (syntactic cue). Prompts such as "Did that make sense and start with the sound you said?" helped students figure out how words work within the sentence rather than in isolation.

> These theories (constructivism) helped professionals realize the importance of using background knowledge and strategy deployment when constructing...word knowledge.

Additionally, advocates of whole language taught phonics instruction through writing. For instance, each day, first-grade teachers began the day with interactive writing, which involved the teacher and students jointly composing a written text. The teacher modeled writing words as students created a sentence or short story. The teacher began writing the story on a chart tablet, saying the letters and sounds as he or she wrote the words. Next, the teacher asked a student to take over writing the words as the other students spelled the words aloud. The teacher read the class-generated story aloud as the students chimed in. Interactive writing provided children with opportunities to hear sounds in words and connect those sounds with corresponding letters and words. Through writing, the reader can become sensitive to written conventions such as letter formation, phonics, and spelling.

Reading Recovery, an early intervention approach for reading, was developed by Clay (1979) during the 1970s in New Zealand and became prevalent in the United States in the 1980s . In Reading Recovery, teachers used writing for sounds to illustrate phonemic segmentation and phonemic synthesis (Clay, 1979). Using the troublesome word, the teacher would write boxes for the sounds in the words. The teacher slowly says the sounds, as the student writes the sounds in the Elkonin boxes (Elkonin, 1973). Then, the student writes this word in the sentence. This approach to phonics found its way into classrooms and helped students learn to use phonemic segmentation and phonemic synthesis to figure out words. Thus, children learned phonics as they wrote. Although the whole-language movement provided an environment rich in social interactions, discussions, high quality literature, student-centered learning, and integration of reading and writing, something more was needed.

Basic research on learning and thinking were paramount during the 1980s, which became the basis for a constructivist view of reading, that is, reading is an active process of building meaning (Pearson & Stephens, 1994; see also chapters 1, 5, 7, and 10, this volume, for more discussion of constructivism). Constructivism and the cognitive view involve an increasing understanding of knowledge of how words are learned. Although basic research on this topic had continued throughout the 1980s (Ehri, 1991), few syntheses had been compiled to give direction for instructional improvements. The debate started again; only this time, it appeared that debate was about the difference between whole language and explicit instruction (Ehri, 1998). The media used this book to rekindle and reformulate the debate in a dichotomous way. The growing debate challenged researchers to clarify multiple ways for teaching phonics. The increased attention set the stage for multiple variations on constructing a knowledge base for phonics. Stahl, Duffy-Hester, and Stahl (1998) declared, "Constructivism is not synonymous with discovery learning, since children can be guided in their constructions more or less explicitly" (p. 350). Thus, children are active learners who can construct a network of phonic knowledge about letters and sounds. Using the theory of constructivism, reading professionals have suggested multiple pathways to teaching phonics. Writing was emphasized, as were spelling-based approaches with teacher demonstration to make the procedures more strategic and explicit. Approaches for systematically teaching decoding by analogy were developed, as well. The following provide examples of the growing multiplicity of approaches to phonics instruction that were developed from a constructivist framework.

Writing

Writing is an important means to develop awareness of the individual sounds in words. As children write, they look closely at how letters are used to form words and construct a system for the spelling (phonic) conventions of written text. As with reading, lots of writing does improve phonic knowledge.

Spelling-Based Approaches

These approaches focused on having children look at the letters in the word and notice the spelling. Two examples follow.

Making Words. Cunningham and colleagues (Cunningham, Hall, & Defee, 1991) developed the Four Blocks Literacy Model, which uses Making Words as one of the key blocks in reading. Making Words is used to help readers develop the ability to spell words and apply this knowledge when decoding. In this procedure, young children learn to make a six- or seven-letter word and the smaller words using a limited number of letter cards. For example, the teacher asks students to take two letters and make the first word, for example *an*. The students make this word, and then the teacher asks them to add an *f*. The

parts of words" (p. 6). Likewise, Stahl and colleagues (1998) found small differences in various phonics programs, but they believed that "it may not matter very much how one conduct(s) phonic instruction" because construction of "knowledge about words may explain why the differences among programs are small" (p. 350). The 1990s ended with a growing consensus that phonics in some way needs to be included in reading instruction. There was renewed support for multiple approaches to teach phonics.

A Brief Look at Phonics in the Early 21st Century

Early into the 21st century, the U.S. federal government enacted the No Child Left Behind (NCLB) Act of 2001, which funded the Reading First initiative (see also chapters 3, 7, 9, and 11, this volume, for further discussion of NCLB and Reading First). Grants became available for schools to purchase programs deemed "scientifically based" for reading instruction in grades K–3. Only programs claiming a "scientific base" defined by experimental studies could be used, which channeled more money into using explicit phonics instruction in beginning reading instruction, often to the exclusion of reading literature and reading information. The implementation of NCLB and Reading First focused on learning phonics by sounding out words letter by letter. Publishers repackaged their 1970s programs and touted them as explicit approaches to teaching phonics (Allington, 2002). There have been numerous investigations regarding the funding of programs. In fact, today there is a growing resistance to the structured one-way approach to phonics instruction that was adopted during the Reading First movement. The winds of change are blowing stronger: Large-scale studies are being conducted on programs such as the Four-Blocks Literacy Model, including Making Words (see page 45–46), to determine their effects on learning to read as well as learning the alphabetic principle. New research has supported a "more contextualized approach that allows teachers to differentiate instruction" (Craig, 2003, p. 38). Furthermore, it appears that writing instruction that encourages phonemic segmentation and invented spellings provides a rich context for developing alphabetic knowledge (Craig, 2003).

I hope that during this decade decoding by analogy and writing will gain greater support for teaching phonics. One program that focuses on using analogies begins with reading a predictable book with rime patterns. The teacher points out the onset and rime patterns in the story, then students rewrite the predictable book using new rimes (Smith, 2002; Walker, 2008). Research in

to teach phonics, thus adding to our repertoire. Using rime analogy is another practice that promotes decoding analogies. Rather than a single pathway, multiple pathways seem an important consideration for dealing with individual differences in learning to decode words. Today, and in the future, professionals will teach phonics by having readers actively figure out words along with others, including the teacher, to create their own system for word learning.

Learning to read is a challenge for many children and should be a concern for all citizens. Conversely, for young children, figuring out words is often both mystery and magic. As professionals, we need to give young children clues to the mystery and celebrate the magic of learning words.

ESSENTIAL READINGS ON PHONICS INSTRUCTION

Anderson, R.C., Hiebert, E.H., Scott, J.A., & Wilkinson, I.A.G. (1985). *Becoming a nation of readers: The report of the Commission on Reading.* Washington, DC: National Institute of Education.

Goswami, U., & Bryant, P. (1990). *Phonological skills and learning to read.* Hillsdale, NJ: Erlbaum.

Juel, C., & Minden-Cupp, C. (2000). Learning to read words: Linguistic units and instructional strategies. *Reading Research Quarterly, 35,* 458–493.

Knapp, M.S. (1995). *Teaching for meaning in high-poverty classrooms.* New York: Teachers College Press.

Stahl, S.A., Duffy-Hester, A.M., & Stahl, K.A.D. (1998). Everything you wanted to know about phonics (but were afraid to ask). *Reading Research Quarterly, 33,* 338–355.

REFERENCES

Adams, M.J. (1990). *Beginning to read: Thinking and learning about print.* Cambridge, MA: MIT Press.

Allington, R. (2002). Troubling times: A short historical perspective. In R. Allington (Ed.), *Big brother and the national reading curriculum: How ideology trumped evidence* (pp. 3–46). Portsmouth, NH: Heinemann.

Anderson, R.C., Hiebert, E.H., Scott, J.A., & Wilkinson, I.A.G. (1985). *Becoming a nation of readers: The report of the Commission on Reading.* Washington, DC: National Institute of Education.

Bear, D.R., Invernizzi, M., Templeton, S., & Johnston, F. (1996). *Words their way: Word study for phonics, vocabulary, and spelling instruction.* Upper Saddle River, NJ: Prentice Hall.

Beery, A. (1949). Development of reading vocabulary and word recognition. In N. Henry (Ed.), *Reading in the elementary school* (48th yearbook of the National Society for the Study of Education, Part II, pp. 172–192). Chicago, IL: National Society for the Study of Education.

(Eds.), *The first R: Every child's right to read* (pp. 259–274). New York: Teachers College Press; Newark, DE: International Reading Association.

Pearson, P.D. (1997). The first-grade studies: A personal reflection. *Reading Research Quarterly, 32*, 428–432.

Pearson, P.D., & Dole, J. (1987). Explicit comprehension instruction: A review of research and a new conceptualization of instruction. *The Elementary School Journal, 88*, 151–165.

Pearson, P.D., & Stephens, D. (1994). Learning about literacy: A 30-year journey. In R. Ruddell, M.R. Ruddell, & H. Singer (Eds.), *Theoretical models and processes of reading* (4th ed., pp. 22–42). Newark, DE: International Reading Association.

Ruddell, R., & Singer, H. (Eds.). (1977). *Theoretical models and processes of reading* (2nd ed.). Newark, DE: International Reading Association.

Skinner, B.F. (1958). Teaching machines. *Science, 128*, 969–977.

Skinner, B.F. (1965). *Science and human behavior.* New York: Free Press.

Smith, M.L. (2002). *The effects of rhyme-rime connection training on second-grade reading performance.* Unpublished dissertation, Oklahoma State University, Stillwater.

Smith, N.B. (1963). *Reading instruction for today's children.* Upper Saddle River, NJ: Prentice Hall.

Snow, C.E., Burns, M.S., & Griffin, P. (Eds.). (1998). *Preventing reading difficulties in young children.* Washington, DC: National Academy Press.

Stahl, S.A., Duffy-Hester, A.M., & Stahl, K.A.D. (1998). Everything you wanted to know about phonics (but were afraid to ask). *Reading Research Quarterly, 33*, 338–355.

Stauffer, R.G. (1970). *The language-experience approach to the teaching of reading.* New York: Harper & Row.

Van Allen, R. (1976). *Language experiences in communication.* Boston: Houghton Mifflin.

Walker, B. (2008). *Diagnostic teaching of reading: Techniques for instruction and assessment* (6th ed.). Upper Saddle River, NJ: Merrill/Pearson.

Walton, P.D. (1995). Rhyming ability, phoneme identity, letter-sound knowledge, and the use of orthographic analogy by prereaders. *Journal of Educational Psychology, 87*, 587–597.

Walton, P.D., Walton, L.M., & Felton, K. (2001). Teaching rime analogy or letter recoding reading strategies to prereaders: Effects on prereading skills and word reading. *Journal of Educational Psychology, 93*, 160–180.

White, T.G. (2005). Effects of systematic and strategic analogy-based phonics on grade 2 students' word reading and reading comprehension. *Reading Research Quarterly, 40*, 234–255.

Williams, J. (1984). Reading instruction today. In A. Harris & E. Sipay (Eds.), *Readings on reading instruction* (3rd ed., pp. 12–19). New York: Longman.

For nearly 50 years, and certainly since the publication of Durkin's (1966) landmark study *Children Who Read Early*, educators, others who interact with families, and even policymakers have increasingly come to see literacy development in families as worth attention. Family literacy advocates point out that two factors related to parents have a significant influence on children's school achievement: parental education and home literacy practices (Paratore, 2003). Family literacy programs are successful models for helping undereducated parents reach their own educational goals (Padak & Rasinski, 2003). But these beliefs are relatively new in education.

In a historical review of advice from reading methods texts about parental involvement in children's education, Sturtevant and Linek (1995) note that early in the 20th century, reading instruction "came to be viewed as a technical skill.... Methods textbooks in this era prepared teachers for this technical task, with the implicit assumption that parents would not be knowledgeable enough to help" (p. 235). Concurrently, most educators believed that children could not learn to read successfully until they were of a sufficient mental age, as measured by the newly available IQ tests, and that parents' meddling with reading could actually harm the child: "Parents will find it hard to realize that irreparable harm might be done to their child if...forced to tackle that job [reading] before reliable tests indicate that he [or she] is ready to do so" (Sturtevant & Linek, 1995, p. 235).

In the 1970s, attitudes and beliefs about poverty and cultural and linguistic differences affected advice teachers were given about parental involvement. Two examples from methods texts published in 1970 illustrate these beliefs:

> Children who come from homes of low cultural level do not have normal opportunities to develop an adequate language background.... They often find it hard to progress in reading even when they have normal intelligence. If they are dull—and many of them are—they are doubly handicapped. (Harris, 1970, p. 33)

> Less privileged children...have lower IQs, are less proficient in language...and are less interested in school.... Their cultural horizons rarely extend beyond the city alleys and, because of this, they cannot bring meaningful concepts to the symbols on the printed page. (Dechant, 1970, pp. 41–42)

Views about family literacy and parental involvement in children's education have certainly changed radically in the past 50 years. Most current scholars agree with Paratore (2003), who notes that family literacy programs "may provide children with a better starting point for learning.... [I]t is likely that we will need to conceptualize parents and children as learning partners well into the elementary school years" (p. 25). We agree. In fact, we believe that finding successful methods of fostering these learning partnerships among students, their

engagement of their children in copying and participating in self-initiated writing projects. In addition, Durkin noted interest in words as the child and parent participated in the reading and rereading of books. Parents answered questions about whole words from television and environmental print, also. Even older siblings were involved, such as by playing school with younger siblings.

The growth in literacy of a young child is strongly related to the family. In highlighting what was important from these studies, Durkin (1966) asserted

> the presence of parents who spend time with their children; who read to them; who answer their questions and their requests for help; and who demonstrate in their own lives that reading is a rich source of relaxation, information, and contentment. (p. 136)

These studies did not show a relationship between early reading and socioeconomic backgrounds. However, parents' attitudes were important. Early readers had parents who were more willing to help their child and were secure in their role as teacher. They did not believe reading had to be in the hands of a trained individual. They responded to their child's interest in reading, and this desire lessened the parents' feeling that they needed "special training" (Durkin, 1966, p. 135).

In contrast, "a third of the nonearly readers who showed preschool interest in reading received no help from their parents" (Durkin, 1966, p. 135). If early help was orchestrated for the nonreaders, it was because of a decision of the parent as opposed to a response to the interest or desire of the child (see also chapters 4 and 5, this volume, for more discussion of Durkin's works).

Hart and Risley: A 30-Million Word Gap by Age 3

Family literacy and early childhood professionals typically encourage parents to talk with their young children to foster their language development and concept learning. However, many children, particularly those who live in poverty, arrive at schools with language delays that eventually affect their success in learning to read and write.

Betty Hart and Todd Risley wanted to learn more about the early language interactions in families of varying socioeconomic status (SES). In the early 1990s, they conducted a study to learn about "what typically went on...with...children learning to talk" (2003, p. 4). They worked with 42 Kansas families over 2½ years. Families differed in socioeconomic status (13 upper SES, 10 middle SES, 13 lower SES, 6 on welfare). The 19 boys and 23 girls in these families were 7–9 months old at the beginning of the study and 3 years old

child. In brief, she found that "Having parents teach specific literacy skills to their children was two times more effective than having parents listen to their children read and six times more effective than encouraging parents to read to their children" (p. i). This major finding held despite children's grade level, reading ability, or socioeconomic status.

In making this claim, Sénéchal noted the relatively small amount of experimental research available to examine effects of shared reading. She excluded important correlational studies from analysis (e.g., Bus, van Ijzendoorn, & Pellegrini [1995], who statistically linked reading acquisition to parent–child book reading). In addition, focus of interventions (e.g., alphabet teaching, word reading, comprehension) in parents' instruction studies varied, so she concluded that particular interventions need further investigation. Thus, this aspect of her work provides important guidance for researchers. Nevertheless, the results of this study show that parental involvement does have a positive impact on children's reading acquisition. Moreover, results offer guidance to practitioners: Teaching parents to teach their children was a more effective intervention than teaching parents to listen to their children read.

> Teaching parents to teach their children was a more effective intervention than teaching parents to listen to their children read.

Together, these studies point us toward the future. From Durkin and from Hart and Risley, we know that what happens in the home makes a difference, for better or for worse. From Sénéchal, we learn that family involvement programs can affect children's reading achievement and that particular emphases seem to yield the most positive results. Yet, like many other programs and practices aimed at providing support for undereducated people or families living in poverty, most family literacy programs are supported with public funds. Thus, no discussion of family literacy would be complete without a look at political influences, which we summarize next.

Political Influences

In the United States, some federal money goes directly to family literacy programs, but most financial support goes to states, which then distribute funds to local programs. The historical genesis of many of these programs was President Lyndon Johnson's War on Poverty (National Public Radio, www.npr.org/templates/story/story.php?storyId=1589660, n.d.). For example, both Head Start and Title I, which have requirements about parental involvement, began in the mid-1960s as part of this effort to reduce or eliminate poverty.

Adequate, stable public funding will probably always be a concern for family literacy professionals. Moreover, funders' reporting requirements and expectations may influence program quality (Padak et al., 2002). How programs and participants are assessed, which we discuss in the following section, seems to be a major issue in this regard.

Assessment Issues

Since continued funding often depends on evidence of participants' progress, assessment and evaluation are important parts of family literacy programs. Programs that receive public funding are required to report learner progress via standardized test results. Alternative assessments such as portfolio evaluation, checklists, observations, and interviews with parents and/or children can show progress in areas that standardized tests cannot. Unfortunately, funding limitations often affect assessment and evaluation activities. As Padak and Baycich (2003) note, "For the most part, family literacy evaluation is in its infancy.... [M]any programs have only minimal evaluation methods in place" (p. 264).

As noted in the previous section, federal funding for Even Start family literacy programs is currently in jeopardy; assessment and evaluation are the culprits. In brief, this situation has arisen from the third national evaluation of Even Start (St. Pierre et al., 2003), which led to the federal Office of Management and Budget (OMB) to label Even Start as "ineffective." The OMB (2005) noted, "National evaluations show the program to have no impact" (paragraph 1).

This strong and negative statement had the predicted effect on many in the federal government. However, according to many family literacy scholars, the OMB's conclusion was inappropriate because measures used in the evaluation were unreliable, data were collected haphazardly, and the design was flawed (see, for example, Goodling Institute, 2003). This situation points to an assessment issue that many programs face: How, often on a shoestring budget, do we design, conduct, and report on evaluation studies that provide valid results in a format accessible to noneducators, such as funders?

Another significant assessment issue relates to the issue of so-called soft skills, such as a parent's increased understanding of or pride in a child's literacy abilities or belief in himself or herself as the child's teacher. Family literacy professionals know the importance of these outcomes, but convincing others, particularly funders, has been problematic. The National Institute for Literacy sponsored several discussion lists. In 2003, Padak and Baycich examined the

Final Thoughts

We need to embrace the complexity of family literacy and find ways to examine both its parts and the phenomenon as a whole. We need to expand our notions of the sites for children's literacy instruction to embrace the potential of outside-of-school activities and programs. We need to find ways to develop authentic partnerships with parents and other adults with whom children interact outside of school hours. Overcoming these challenges will allow us to determine the actual impact of family literacy on children's and parents' literacy growth.

ESSENTIAL READINGS ON FAMILY LITERACY

Assessment

Assessment and Evaluation Strategies in Family Literacy Program Development: www.nald.ca/clr/aestrat/cover.htm

Synthesis of Local and State Even Start Evaluations: www.ed.gov/pubs/evenstart_final/synthesis/synthesisa_h.html

Holt, D., & VanDuzer, C. (Eds.). (2000). *Assessing success in family literacy and adult ESL*. Washington, DC: Center for Applied Linguistics.

Research Reviews

Gadsden, V.L. (2000). Intergenerational literacy within families. In M.L. Kamil, P.B. Mosenthal, P.D. Pearson, & R. Barr (Eds.), *Handbook of reading research* (Vol. 3, pp. 871–887). Mahwah, NJ: Erlbaum.

Nickse, R. (1990). *Family and intergenerational literacy programs: An update of "The Noises of Literacy"* (Information Series No. 342). Columbus, OH: ERIC Clearinghouse on Adult, Career, and Vocational Education. (ERIC Document Reproduction Service No. ED327736)

Padak, N., & Rasinski, T. (2003). *Family literacy: Who benefits?* Kent, OH: Ohio Literacy Resource Center. Retrieved January 20, 2007, from literacy.kent.edu/Oasis/Pubs/WhoBenefits2003.pdf

Padak, N., Sapin, C., & Baycich, D. (2002). *A decade of family literacy: Programs, outcomes, and future prospects*. Columbus, OH: ERIC Clearinghouse on Adult, Career, and Vocational Education. (ERIC Document Reproduction Service No. ED465074)

Purcell-Gates, V. (2000). Family literacy. In M.L. Kamil, P.B. Mosenthal, P.D. Pearson, & R. Barr (Eds.), *Handbook of reading research* (Vol. 3, pp. 853–870). Mahwah, NJ: Erlbaum.

(pp. 99–122). Albany: State University of New York Press.

St. Pierre, R., Ricciuti, A., Tao, F., Creps, C., Swartz, J., Lee, W., et al. (2003). *Third national Even Start evaluation: Program impacts and implications for improvement*. Washington, DC: US Department of Education.

Sturtevant, E.G., & Linek, W.M. (1995). Parents and teachers working together toward literacy: Views from the past and goals for the future. *Reading and Writing Quarterly*, *11*, 233–245.

U.S. Department of Education. (2002). *William F. Goodling Even Start family literacy programs*. Retrieved January 21, 2007, from www.ed.gov/policy/elsec/leg/esea02/pg6.html

Michael F. Opitz

I was taken by surprise when guided reading became all the rage in the 1990s. It seemed to me that the topic was not really a new one, because as a first-grade teacher, I had used guided reading since the mid-1970s. I wondered if I had missed something along the way or if there might be new information that I could and should share with the prospective teachers I was now charged to teach at the university. I read the newest information about guided reading, attended conference sessions, and presented on the topic myself. Through all of this professional activity, I discovered that there are common elements to lessons that carry the guided reading label and that many of the seeds for the guided reading of today were planted several years ago. I also discovered that the problems of the past were becoming the problems of today. I began to see children locked into leveled groups. I listened to children talk about reading and their focus on the mention of reading level rather than authors and titles. I began to hear comments such as "All children need literature circles, but struggling readers need guided reading." Surely, I thought, there has to be a way to keep the good parts of guided reading, then and now, and ditch the rest. The search began and still continues.

Guided reading is perhaps one of the most common elements of today's reading programs. Most descriptions of comprehensive literacy programs now include guided reading as one of the essential components (Cunningham, Hall, & Cunningham, 2000; Fountas & Pinnell, 1996). Although there is a tendency to view it as a fairly new practice, it is anything but revolutionary. This is not to say that guided reading has remained exactly the same over the years, that it was used for the same reasons, or that it was used with the same intensity. All three have fluctuated throughout time. In this chapter, we take a look at 50 years of guided reading by examining representative influential writers whose work has been used to teach teachers how to teach reading. Several of these authors were also authors of the commercial materials (i.e., basal readers) that were mass produced and used to teach children. The ideas they set forth in their textbooks, then, found their way into the materials that teachers used to teach children.

Table 4.1. Directed Reading Activity

Step	Purpose
1. Prepare students for reading the selection	• To ascertain students' background for the given text • To help students build background for the text if none or little exists • To help students relate their backgrounds to the story at hand, thereby creating interest and reading for meaning • To help children make connections with previous stories • To help children with any unique words they might encounter • To establish a purpose for reading
2. Silent reading of the selection precedes oral reading	• To get the "wholeness" of the story • To help students learn to apply what they know to decode unknown words and to apply comprehension skills, asking for help when necessary
3. Rereading, either silent or oral, for new purposes	• To promote fluency, foster rhythmical reading, and to relate details to the big idea
4. Follow-up activities to meet the needs and interests of students	• To develop organization skills and promote efficient study habits

Based on Betts (1946, pp. 430–431).

Table 4.2. Step 2: Guided Reading

Teaching Procedure	Purpose
1. Ask the major motivating question	• Helps the children see a reason or purpose for reading
2. Ask other questions to guide the children through the story	• Helps children have a purpose for reading a given part of the story • Depending on question, helps children to read silently, to visualize character, scene, and action • Helps build self-reliance because the children rely on themselves to find answers to questions • When asked to read answers to questions, helps children to satisfy their need to achieve and to share
3. Answer the major motivating question	• Meets the child's need to resolve tension by finding the answer to a question

Based on Gray and Reese (1957, p. 156).

nique to use with small groups to a way of defining small-group instruction. Fountas and Pinnell identified these essential elements of guided reading:

- Teacher works with children in small groups who are similar in their development and are able to read approximately the same level of text
- Teacher introduces the stories and assists children's reading in ways that help to develop reading strategies so children can reach the goal of being able to read independently and silently
- Each child reads whole texts with an emphasis on reading increasingly challenging books over time
- Children are grouped and regrouped in a dynamic process that involves ongoing observation and assessment (p. 4)

Since then, many others have defined essential elements of guided reading (see Booth, 1998; Calkins, 2000; Cunningham, Hall, & Cunningham, 2000; Opitz & Ford, 2001; Routman, 2000). Regardless of decade or author, all agree that guided reading is planned, intentional, focused instruction when the teacher helps students, usually in small-group settings, learn more about the reading process.

What Has Caused Guided Reading to Change?

The history of guided reading has been significantly affected by the role and nature of small-group instruction in elementary reading programs. Small-group reading instruction organized with homogenous-ability groups was the predominant feature of elementary reading programs during most of the past 50 years (Caldwell & Ford, 2002). The infamous three reading groups—high, middle, and low—with not-so-subtle names—bluebirds, robins, and crows, for example—were pervasive in reading classrooms. Research, however, revealed that grouping children by so-called ability was fraught with problems (Barr, 1995; Opitz, 1998). Research-based concerns documenting arbitrary selection standards, inequitable access to quality meaning-based instruction, and long-lasting negative social stigma, however, did little to derail this questionable practice.

The problems with this practice had less to do with the actual grouping format and more to do with the nature of instruction during the small-group time. The type of guided instruction advocated by Betts and others rarely captured the typical instruction in ability groups, even when teachers were using the basal materials these experts were involved in designing. In her classic study of comprehension instruction, Durkin (1978/1979) observed that small-group instruction was basal-driven. Teacher-directed, round-robin oral reading followed by literal-level questions was the type of instruction often found in small groups.

sources for teaching children to read. Most often authors wrote stories for the basal using a given number of words per story. While basal readers continue to be the mainstay of the reading material used to teach reading, the content is quite different. Some include children's literature, either the entire book or a chapter from the book. As guided reading has gained popularity, basal reading programs have begun including separately packaged sets of leveled readers specifically designed for this aspect of reading programs.

Some changes are more subtle. A veteran teacher recently asked, "Weren't the reading groups we used in the past leveled? How is this any different from what we used to do?" Clearly the difference is not in the size or make-up of the groups. This teacher's question surfaces a concern we share: If teachers subscribe to a view of guided reading that emphasizes the use of text levels as the primary way to group children, what we frequently see is a return to ability grouping. Even when teachers go beyond text levels, guided reading groups can become static. When we rely on ability grouping in guided reading, we are apt to create problems. One problem that could resurface is the debilitating effects of labeling. Continual reference to these levels could work to label—and stigmatize—the groups in much the same way the traditional labels (bluebirds, robins, and crows) of years past did.

So how do we prevent the return of these problems? The difference needs to be the nature of the instruction provided in the small homogenous groups (Hornsby, 2000; Schulman & DaCruz Payne, 2000). Theoretically we see a significant shift from transmission models of learning to transactional models of learning. Instruction moves from being based on skill-based behaviorism to strategy-based constructivism. The key focus is no longer on covering materials. It is on teaching learners. Assessment is an ongoing process that informs decisions about who to teach, what to teach, what materials to use, and how to teach what is needed. Assessment-informed instruction should mean that small groups in guided reading will be organized in a much more fluid, flexible manner avoiding the static, fixed memberships of the ability groups of the past (The Wright Group, 1996).

The very term *guided* suggests a type of instruction that would be less about teachers transmitting information and more about teachers coaching students. This difference is especially critical when research reveals that the frequent use of "coaching during reading" may be one of the most significant distinctions between highly effective schools and moderately or less effective schools (Taylor, Pearson, Clark, & Walpole, 1999, p. 158). In instructional models that advocate a gradual release of responsibility (Au & Raphael, 1998; Pearson &

1. All children have the ability to become literate. Every child is ready to learn something. Our job as teachers is to determine what the child already knows and what the child needs to learn, then to design instruction accordingly.

2. All children need to be taught by a skilled teacher in order to maximize their full potential in reading. Good teaching matters every step of the way. This is especially true for those children who need our help the most. Snow, Burns, and Griffin (1998) comment,

> Children who are having difficulty learning to read do not, as a rule, require qualitatively different instruction from children who are "getting it." Instead, they more often need application of the same principles by someone who can apply them expertly to individual children who are having difficulty for one reason or another. (p. 12)

3. The goal of guided reading is to help children become independent readers. The whole purpose of providing children with guided reading experiences is to help them become independent readers as quickly as possible.

4. Guided reading is but one component of an effective reading program. Guided reading should show children how to read and should provide a scaffold (i.e., support) for them as they read. An effective literacy program also includes reading aloud by the teacher, as well as shared reading and independent reading by students. Elements of the reading program are enhanced by comparable elements in the writing program and the use of content instruction as additional opportunities for reading–writing strategies.

5. Reading for meaning is the primary goal of guided reading. The instruction is designed to help children construct meaning. Betts (1946) noted years ago,

> During the first reading the child is encouraged to ask for any kind of help he needs. To stimulate interest, to enlist effort, and to cause the child to come to grips with the meaning, this silent reading is guided by suggestions, comments, and questions. (p. 508)

6. Children learn to read by reading. Children need to do much reading at their independent and instructional levels to become competent readers. There is general agreement that when children read with 95–100% word accuracy and 75–100% comprehension, they are reading at their *independent level*. When children read with 91–94% word accuracy and 60–75% comprehension, they are reading at their *instructional level*. At the same time, we must acknowledge the complexity of variables that intersect when an individual comprehends. A child might very well be reading a book well beyond his or her "level" one day and the next day struggle with an "on level" book. Many factors contribute to the

they most often want to repeat the experience, which provides meaningful, purposeful practice that leads to a favorable view of reading (Cullinan, 1992; Gambrell, 1996; Opitz, 1995; Watson, 1997).

11. Specific elements characterize the successful guided reading lesson. It relies on a three-part lesson plan (Before/During/After Reading) with one focal point for the overall lesson and the use of specific teaching strategies at each phase of the lesson. Lessons should help children achieve independence with the teacher assisting and assessing individual children as needed. Recognizing that comprehension is the essence of reading and the importance of making sure that students gain this understanding, teachers should also engage children in a discussion about the texts they read (e.g., Fountas & Pinnell, 2001; Opitz & Ford, 2001).

Where Do We See Guided Reading in the Future?

In addition to what we have learned from doing this brief historical sketch of guided reading, our view of the future of guided reading is shaped from extensive involvement in working with educators as they learned about, implemented, and evaluated their use of guided reading. We have also learned much from analyzing results of a recent national survey that asked teachers to discuss issues and ideas related to their practice of guided reading (Ford & Opitz, in press). The responses of over 1,500 primary teachers, despite self-reporting great familiarity with guided reading, revealed to us that we are still struggling with how to effectively implement this new practice so learners gain the most from it. While our perspective on guided reading encompasses many of the commonly accepted understandings, we recommend a wider array of guided reading experiences that open up new learning possibilities for teachers and students alike (Opitz & Ford, 2001). Here are some of the most critical problems we propose for further examination related to the future of guided reading:

1. How do we help educators develop a clearer understanding of the purposes of guided reading to avoid returning to the flawed grouping practices of the past?

2. How do we show educators how to foster connections between guided reading and the other components of the literacy program so that guided reading isn't seen by educators and/or learners as a separate component, minimizing its potential impact and transfer of outcomes to other literacy experiences and contexts?

ed reading creates an instructional tool that more effectively nurtures and supports both reading and readers. As we look toward the future, we are discovering that there may be more than one way to implement effective guided reading instruction.

ESSENTIAL READINGS ON GUIDED READING

Booth, D.W. (1996). *Literacy techniques for building successful readers and writers*. York, ME: Stenhouse/Pembroke.

Booth, D.W. (1998). *Guiding the reading process*. York, ME: Stenhouse.

Calkins, L. (2001). *The art of teaching reading*. New York: Longman.

Cunningham, P.M., & Allington, R.L. (2007). *Classrooms that work: They can all read and write* (4th ed.). Boston: Allyn & Bacon.

Cunningham, P.M., Hall, D.P., & Cunningham, J.W. (2000). *Guided reading the Four Blocks way*. Greensboro, NC: Carson-Dellosa.

Fountas, I.C., & Pinnell, G.S. (1996). *Guided reading: Good first teaching for all children*. Portsmouth, NH: Heinemann.

Fountas, I.C., & Pinnell, G.S. (2001). *Guiding readers and writers, grades 3–6: Teaching comprehension, genre, and content literacy*. Portsmouth, NH: Heinemann.

Mooney, M. (1990). *Reading to, with, and by children*. New York: Richard C. Owen.

Opitz, M.F., & Ford, M.P. (2001). *Reaching readers: Flexible and innovative strategies for guided reading*. Portsmouth, NH: Heinemann.

Routman, R. (2000). *Conversations: Strategies for teaching, learning, and evaluating*. Portsmouth, NH: Heinemann.

REFERENCES

Alexander, P.A., & Jetton, T.L. (2000). Learning from text: A multidimensional and developmental perspective. In M.L. Kamil, P. Mosenthal, P.D. Pearson, & R. Barr (Eds.), *Handbook of reading research* (Vol. 3, pp. 285–310). Mahwah, NJ: Erlbaum.

Anderson, R.C., Hiebert, E.H., Scott, J.A., & Wilkinson, I.A.G. (1985). *Becoming a nation of readers: The report of the Commission on Reading*. Washington, DC: National Institute of Education.

Au, K.H., & Raphael, T.E. (1998). Curriculum and teaching in a literature-based program. In T. Raphael & K. Au (Eds.), *Literature-based instruction: Reshaping the curriculum* (pp. 123–148). Norwood, MA: Christopher-Gordon.

Barr, R. (1995). What research says about grouping in the past and present and what it suggests for the future. In M.C. Radencich & L.J. McKay (Eds.), *Flexible grouping for literacy in the elementary grades* (pp. 1–24). Boston: Allyn & Bacon.

Betts, E.A. (1946). *Foundations of reading instruction*. New York: American Book Company.

Snow, C., Burns, M.S., & Griffin, P. (1998). *Preventing reading difficulties in young children.* Washington, DC: National Academy Press.

Spache, G.D., & Spache, E. (1986). *Reading in the elementary school* (5th ed.). Boston: Allyn & Bacon.

Taylor, B.M., Pearson, P.D., Clark, K.F., & Walpole, S. (1999). Effective schools/accomplished teachers. *The Reading Teacher, 53,* 156–159.

Watson, D. (1997). Beyond decodable texts: Supportive and workable literature. *Language Arts, 74,* 635–643.

Wilhelm, J.D. (2001). *Improving comprehension with think-aloud strategies.* New York: Scholastic.

Wong, B.Y.L., & Jones, W. (1982). Increasing metacomprehension in learning disabled and normally achieving students through self-questioning training. *Learning Disability Quarterly, 5,* 228–240.

The Wright Group. (1996). *Guided reading level 1: Guiding students from emergent literacy to independence.* Bothell, WA: Author.

Today, comprehension, along with phonemic awareness, phonics, fluency, and vocabulary, is one of the five building blocks of literacy (National Institute of Child Health and Human Development, 2000). There are a variety of texts that support research-based comprehension practices (Barone & Morrow, 2002; Block, Gambrell, & Pressley, 2002; Block & Pressley, 2002; Farstrup & Samuels, 2002; International Reading Association, 2002) and a number of volumes about teaching reading comprehension strategies (Blachowicz & Ogle, 2001; Buehl, 2001; Harvey & Goudvis, 2000; McLaughlin & Allen, 2002). I should note at this point that although comprehension is listed as one of the five emphases, it is perceived to be the ultimate goal. Phonemic awareness, phonics, fluency, and vocabulary all contribute to comprehension.

There has not always been such an emphasis placed on reading comprehension, but, nonetheless, the past 50 years of research and practice have provided a context for how we perceive comprehension today. In this chapter, the focus is on what we have learned about reading comprehension in the past half century and what directions future research might take. It opens with a widely accepted definition of reading comprehension, followed by a review of five decades of selected research and its relation to practice. The chapter concludes with suggestions about what directions future reading comprehension research might take.

How Is Reading Comprehension Defined?

Although there are many different definitions of reading comprehension today, most appear to support the constructivist nature of the definition proposed by Harris and Hodges (1995) in *The Literacy Dictionary:*

> The construction of meaning of a written or spoken communication through a reciprocal, holistic interchange of ideas between the interpreter and the message in a particular communicative context. *Note:* The presumption here is that meaning resides in the intentional problem-solving, thinking processes of the interpreter during such an interchange, that the content of meaning is influenced by that person's prior knowledge and experience, and that the message so constructed by the receiver may or may not be congruent with the message sent. (p. 39)

Anderson's work on schema theory (1984), which suggests that prior knowledge and experience affect readers' understanding, is embedded in this definition (see also chapters 1 and 7, this volume, for discussion of schema theory).

An evolution of reading comprehension has occurred through the decades. We have moved from a time when comprehension was not emphasized to a time when it is a national focus of reading instruction. A half century of history

When considering reading at this point in history, Singer (1985) noted that prior to the 1950s, research in reading in the United States was mostly atheoretical. He viewed Holmes's Substrata Factor Theory (1953) as a landmark contribution to the field and described it in this way:

> Underlying each of reading's two components, speed and power (comprehension), are a multiplicity of skills and processes; the reader organizes them into momentary working systems according to his or her purposes and the demands of the task. This view of reading explains why different methods of reading instruction work. Each emphasizes one or more subsystems necessary for reading. As readers progress through school, their individual differences decrease in perceptual components of reading and increase in cognitive and linguistic subsystems. (p. 12)

More than two decades later, LaBerge and Samuels (1976) would theorize that processing print at an automatic rate enables readers to give more of their attention to reading comprehension.

When the 1960s began, many of the practices of the previous decade remained common practice, but as the decade progressed, reading came to be viewed as a perceptual process. Graphic symbols on a printed page were translated into an oral code. Comprehension was comprehension of speech produced by the reader. Reading was a perceptual process that, when accompanied by a translation process, produced a linguistic code that was treated by the brain as a language process (Pearson & Stephens, 1994).

This was also the decade in which other disciplines began studying reading. This may seem unusual, but it makes sense when we consider that every discipline uses reading, and, consequently, every discipline values comprehension. The psychologists, sociologists, psycholinguists, and sociolinguists developed their own perspectives of reading and the field became transdisciplinary. For example, the linguists, represented by Fries (1963) and others, supported the ideas that reading was closely aligned with writing, speaking, and listening. Fries's publication *Linguistics and Reading* delineated the Linguistic Perspective.

Another linguist, Chomsky (1965), focused his work on language acquisition and a belief that language was rule-governed. He believed that children were predisposed to language because they had innate language acquisition devices. He espoused that children were active participants in language and created their own theories about it, as they tested their hypotheses (see chapters 1, 2, 6, and 10, this volume, for more discussion of Chomsky's influence).

Psycholinguistics, a new field of inquiry, emerged in the 1960s. Ken Goodman, a highly influential researcher, represented this perspective. His articles "A Linguistic Study of Cues and Miscues in Reading" (1965) and

Finally, Braunger and Lewis (2006) note that the idea of emergent literacy was coined by Marie Clay in 1966. This contribution was significant because it described behaviors of very young children as they began to respond to approximate reading and writing acts. *Emergent literacy* focused on how children learn, while, in contrast, *readiness* was viewed as a set of tasks developed by adults to represent learning . The concept of emergent literacy helped us to understand how children begin to comprehend (see also chapters 2 and 4, this volume, for more discussion of Clay's influence). It would, however, be years before *emergent literacy* would become a commonly used term in the reading profession and the object of studies by such notable researchers as Lesley Mandel Morrow (2000) and Dorothy Strickland (1998).

Leading Researchers and Influential Publications of the 1970s

During the 1970s, several prominent researchers emerged. These included Frank Smith, Walter Kintsch, David Rumelhart, Louise Rosenblatt, Dolores Durkin, and Lev Vygotsky. The decade also marked the publication of several seminal works.

In 1971, Smith, a psycholinguist, delineated his beliefs in *Understanding Reading: A Psycholinguistic Analysis of Reading and Learning to Read*. In this influential work, Smith argued that reading was something one learned to do—not something one was taught; that reading was only incidentally visual—being able to see was necessary but not sufficient to achieve understanding; that reading was a matter of making informed predictions; that reading was a constructive process—learners made sense of what they read based on what they already knew. In his analysis of Smith's work, Pearson (2000) noted that Smith's ideas revolutionized the reading field. The psycholinguistic perspective, which emerged in the 1960s and underpinned Smith's thinking, encouraged us to value literacy experiences that focused on making meaning, to value texts that used natural language patterns, and to understand the reading process and appreciate children's efforts as readers, and it gave us a means (miscue analysis) and a theory (reading as a constructive process) that were remarkably distinct from previous ideas about reading. In addition, the psycholinguists made explicit links between oral and written language acquisition and helped us view reading as language rather than perception (see also chapters 1, 2, and 9, this volume, for more discussion of the influence of psycholinguistics).

This was also the decade of the Cognitive Revolution, a movement that "brought both knowledge and text structure into leading roles in explaining

In 1978, Rosenblatt also published an important work, *The Reader, the Text, and the Poem: The Transactional Theory of the Literary Work*, in which she suggested that meaning resides in the transaction between the reader and the text—not in the reader's head or on the printed page, as others had previously argued. In her 2002 presentation at the National Reading Conference, Rosenblatt stressed the importance of readers' abilities to think and express their own ideas. While explaining her Aesthetic–Efferent Continuum, Rosenblatt (2002) noted that she used the term *transaction*—not *interaction*—because there was a human being involved. She noted that transaction assumes a mind, an individual existing in a context. The reader is in a social context—including everything he or she has experienced and what he or she is feeling—choosing to read. Transaction implies that readers' personal experiences shape their understanding of text, indicating that response is personal and may vary.

Rosenblatt (2002) suggested that stances were "aspects of consciousness." She believed that if we perceive consciousness as a stream flowing through the darkness, stance might be viewed as a mechanism lighting up or directing attention to various parts of the stream (Rosenblatt, 2004). She further noted that stance "provides the guiding orientation toward activating particular areas and elements of consciousness, that is particular proportions of public and private aspects of meaning (Rosenblatt, 2004, p. 1374). (For a more detailed discussion of stance, see Rosenblatt, 2004.) Rosenblatt's Aesthetic–Efferent Continuum (1994) reflects her belief that readers transact with text from aesthetic and efferent stances. The aesthetic stance depicts a predominantly emotional perspective; the efferent stance, a predominantly factual one. Rosenblatt (2002) noted that no reading experience is purely aesthetic or purely efferent, but rather readers are always making choices about their thinking, focusing on both stances, and sometimes more on one than the other (see also Chapter 1, this volume, for discussion of Rosenblatt's influence).

Implications for the Teaching of Reading Comprehension

Basal reading programs continued to be widely used during the 1970s. These often included ancillary materials for phonics and workbooks that focused on the practice of comprehension skills (i.e., main idea, comparison/contrast, sequencing). Teachers were viewed as classroom managers (Pearson, 1985), who, according to Durkin (1978/1979), did not use very much time teaching reading comprehension. Duffy (2002) observed that Durkin's research inspired studies designed to find ways to improve reading comprehension. The resulting four

Schema theory, like the psycholinguistic perspective, also promoted a constructivist view of comprehension; all readers must, at every moment in the reading process, construct a coherent model of reading for the texts they read. The most important consequence of this constructivist perspective is that there is inherent ambiguity about where meaning resides. (p. 168)

Early in the decade, researchers were just beginning to investigate comprehension as it related to "story structures, integration of sentences, drawing inferences, testing hypotheses, relating background knowledge to textual information, and reading to obtain information" (Guthrie, 1981, p. viii). But by the mid-1980s, it was evident that researcher-developed instruction in reading strategies, such as self-questioning, summarizing, rereading, visualizing, and analyzing story grammar elements could benefit students. In fact, Roehler and Duffy (1984) suggested using direct explanation to teach such strategies. This was also the time that Palincsar and Brown (1984) published "Reciprocal Teaching of Comprehension-Fostering and -Monitoring Activities," suggesting that bundling comprehension strategies could deepen students' understanding.

Further, the importance of metacognition emerged during the 1980s (Paris, Cross, & Lipson, 1984). Metacognition, thinking about thinking, understanding what we know and what we do not know, greatly influenced reading comprehension and learning. Duffy (2002) reported that it was the research on metacognition that inspired studies about helping readers to become conscious of the strategic nature of comprehension. He noted that Question–Answer Relationships (QAR; Raphael, 1986) and reciprocal teaching (Palincsar & Brown, 1984) were two important comprehension routines that were published at this time.

While details about comprehension strategies were emerging, significant developments were also occurring in related areas of teaching and learning. The sociologists made a number of contributions to our understanding of reading during this decade, including increased understanding of dialect. But, more importantly, they encouraged us to think about reading as a social process and introduced an expanded notion of context (Pearson & Stephens, 1994). During the same period, Bruner (1983) was writing about scaffolded teaching and learning, a process in which teachers begin by providing a great deal of support and gradually decrease their input as students become more knowledgeable and more independent. This integrated Vygotsky's (1934/1978) work on the more knowledgeable other and the social nature of learning.

Finally, the whole-language movement emerged in the 1980s. Based on the use of authentic literature and the writing process, and a deemphasis of

Reinking, 1996; Baker & Wigfield, 1999; Guthrie & Alvermann, 1999). Engaged learners achieve because they want to understand, they possess intrinsic motivations for interacting with text, they use cognitive skills to understand, and they share knowledge by talking with teachers and peers (Guthrie & Wigfield, 1997).

In the 1990s, researchers reported a lack of comprehension strategy instruction (Pressley, Wharton-McDonald, Mistretta-Hampton, & Echevarria, 1998). In fact, reading comprehension in general seemed to vanish—perhaps as a result of the lack of emphasis on skills and strategies during the whole-language movement, which preferred to have comprehension emerge from the use of authentic texts (Pearson, 2000). Despite this trend, a seminal publication by Dole, Duffy, Roehler, and Pearson (1991) provided us with comprehension strategies focused on the construction of meaning: prediction, generating questions, determining importance, drawing inferences, and self-monitoring. These would become the foundation of reading strategy instruction. A year later, Pressley and his colleagues introduced us to transactional strategies instruction (TSI), the teaching of self-regulated comprehension processes (Pressley, El-Dinary, & Schuder, 1992). The instruction is transactional among group members, and it features transactions between reader and text and transactions of socially constructed meaning. According to El-Dinary (2002), "TSI teachers and students act as a literary community, using strategies to construct and evaluate interpretations of text" (p. 201).

During this time multiple vocabulary studies informed our thinking. They concluded, among other factors, that vocabulary development and instruction affect reading comprehension (Baumann & Kame'enui, 1991; Beck & McKeown, 1991; Blachowicz & Fisher, 2000). As the National Reading Panel (National Institute of Child Health and Human Development, 2000) has noted, "Reading comprehension is a complex, cognitive process that cannot be understood without a clear description of the role that vocabulary development and vocabulary instruction play in the understanding of what has been read" (p. 13).

In 1996, Almasi described discussions as "forums for collaboratively constructing meaning and for sharing responses" (p. 2). Because of the dynamic nature of these discussions, the meanings readers construct are continually transformed by their experiences, interactions with others, and information from the text. This social interaction is another aspect of literacy that is underpinned by Vygotsky's research (1934/1978).

In 2001, Pearson noted that what we know about teaching comprehension strategies still is not making its way to classroom teachers. This need for professional development is supported by a variety of studies, including primary-grade research in which first-grade students learned to use and regulate reading comprehension strategies after their teachers had engaged in professional development that focused on strategy instruction (Hilden & Pressley, 2002; McLaughlin, 2003).

This was also the time in which critical literacy (Freire, 1970, 1983) became a renewed focus. When we read from a critical stance, we move beyond understanding the text to understanding the power relationship that exists between the reader and the author—to knowing that even though the author has the power to create and present the message, readers have the power and the right to be text critics, to read, question, and analyze the author's message. Understanding this power relationship is the essence of critical literacy. Reading from a critical stance requires both the ability and the deliberate inclination to think critically about—to analyze and evaluate—texts (books, media, lyrics, hypertext, life relationships), to meaningfully question their origin and purpose, and to take action. The goal is for readers to become text critics in everyday life—to comprehend information sources from a critical stance as naturally as they comprehend from the aesthetic and efferent stances.

The early 21st century also gave us the neurobiological approach to reading. As Hamm and Pearson (2002) reported,

> This new area of research enabled by advanced technology, holds promise for sharpening and deepening our understanding of the comprehension process, for it may remove some of the mysteries involved in trying to fathom the relationship among various aspects of the reading process, such as phonological processing, decoding, word meaning, and comprehension. (p. 513)

Implications for the Teaching of Reading Comprehension

In the first seven years of this decade, researchers such as Duke (2001), Dole (2000), Duffy (2002), Pearson (2000, 2001, 2006), and Pressley (2000, 2002, 2006) continued to question the nature of reading comprehension, as well as ways to teach comprehension strategies. The influence of the National Reading Panel report (National Institute of Child Health and Human Development, 2000) was clearly evident, as the five building blocks of reading—phonemic awareness (Ehri & Nunes, 2002), phonics (Stahl, Duffy-Hester, & Stahl, 1998), fluency (Rasinski, 2003), vocabulary (Beck & McKeown, 1991; Blachowicz &

particularly preservice programs that promote diversity, and (d) how to bring a greater number of teachers of diverse backgrounds into the profession. Hoffman and Pearson (2000) agreed that issues of diversity should be emphasized as the reading profession builds a research agenda for teacher preparation in reading.

The Changing Nature of Text

In past decades, texts were limited to materials such as books, articles, contracts, and newspapers, but now the term *text* has expanded meanings. Multiple literacies is a general example of this; critical literacy is a specific example. When engaging in critical literacy, text may refer to trade books, informational articles, textbooks, hypertext, song lyrics, movies, television shows, everyday life situations, and more. The term is so far reaching, because reading from a critical stance permeates every aspect of life (McLaughlin & DeVoogd, 2004). In critical literacy, readers see beyond the situation of the text and examine more deeply the complexities of the text (Wink, 2000).

Understanding the multifaceted nature of text is essential for comprehending at deeper levels. Many of us grew up in a time when the published word was accepted as truth. That is no longer the case. To truly comprehend, readers must now be capable of questioning the author's intent and the publisher's purpose. As Luke and Freebody (1999) noted, readers must play not only the roles of code breakers, meaning makers, and text users but also the role of text critics. Continuing to research the changing nature of text can only enhance our understanding of the role it plays in reading comprehension.

The Expanding Notion of Context

Although the sociologists greatly contributed to our understanding of context, new information continues to emerge. In 2001, Duke delineated an expanded understanding of context for present-day learners. She suggested that context should be viewed as curriculum, activity, classroom environment, teachers and teaching, text, and society.

One of the interesting aspects of the expanded notion of context is how many people, structures, and influences affect student understanding. Cambourne (2002) reminded us that "what is learned cannot be separated from the context in which it is learned" (p. 26). Research that investigates context from this expanded perspective will help us to better understand our teaching, as well as our students.

of literacy and embrace new perspectives. This includes viewing comprehension as a continuous learning process.

The Need for New, More Effective Models of Comprehension

Numerous models of reading, each of which addresses comprehension, have been developed over the past half century. Examples featured in the fifth edition of *Theoretical Models and Processes of Reading* (Ruddell & Unrau, 2004b) include cognitive processing models (Adams, 2004; Kintsch, 2004; Rumelhart, 2004; Samuels, 2004), the dual coding model (Sadoski & Paivio, 2004), the transactional model (Rosenblatt, 2004), the attitude-influence model (Mathewson, 2004), and the sociocognitive model (Ruddell & Unrau, 2004a). Hamm and Pearson (2002) also discussed the most recent neurobiological approach, but one of the conclusions they derived from examining reading approaches through the decades was that there is no one approach that provides an adequate account of comprehension.

In light of the existing research, Pearson (2006) recently created a new model of comprehension, the "Situation Model," based on the Construction–Integration Comprehension Model of Walter Kintsch. This is a mental model that accounts for all the facts and resources available in the current situation. The model integrates world knowledge, topical knowledge, disciplinary knowledge, and linguistic knowledge, focusing on the knowledge–comprehension relation. Readers use their knowledge to build a Situation Model for a text. The information in the Situation Model is then available to become part of their long-term memory and store of knowledge. And, as Pearson noted, "Knowledge begets comprehension begets knowledge."

As time progresses and we learn more about human capabilities, particularly brain functions, our understanding of reading, and particularly reading comprehension, will continue to evolve. Reading researchers, such as those noted in this section, will lead the way to our increased understanding.

Final Thoughts

Reading and, consequently, reading comprehension have changed and changed again over the past five decades. Our field has expanded, our knowledge has grown, and our understanding has deepened. We have witnessed advances in research and their eventual integration into practice. We have also taught through a variety of instructional movements that have brought us to this time of balanced literacy.

Irwin, J.W., & Doyle, M.A. (Eds.). (1992). *Reading/writing connections: Learning from research*. Newark, DE: International Reading Association.

Kamil, M.L., Mosenthal, P., Pearson, P.D., & Barr, R. (Eds.). (2000). *Handbook of reading research* (Vol. 3). Mahwah, NJ: Erlbaum. (multiple chapters)

Pearson, P.D. (2000). Reading in the twentieth century. In T. Good (Ed.), *American education: Yesterday, today, and tomorrow* (Yearbook of the National Society for the Study of Education, pp. 152–208). Chicago: University of Chicago Press.

Pearson, P.D., & Stephens, D. (1994). Learning about literacy: A 30-year journey. In R.B. Ruddell, M.R. Ruddell, & H. Singer (Eds.), *Theoretical models and processes of reading* (4th ed., pp. 22–42). Newark, DE: International Reading Association.

Pressley, M. (2006, April 29). *What the future of reading research could be*. Paper presented at the International Reading Association Reading Research 2006 conference, Chicago, IL.

Ruddell, R.B., & Unrau, N.J. (Eds.). (2004). *Theoretical models and processes of reading* (5th ed.). Newark, DE: International Reading Association. (multiple chapters)

REFERENCES

Adams, M.J. (2004). Modeling the connections between word recognition and reading. In R.B. Ruddell & N.J. Unrau (Eds.), *Theoretical models and processes of reading* (5th ed., pp. 1219–1243). Newark, DE: International Reading Association.

Almasi, J.F. (1996). A new view of discussion. In L.B. Gambrell & J.F. Almasi (Eds.), *Lively discussions! Fostering engaged reading* (pp. 2–24). Newark, DE: International Reading Association.

Anderson, R.C. (1984). Some reflections on the acquisition of knowledge. *Educational Researcher, 13*, 5–10.

Anderson, R.C., & Pearson, P.D. (1984). A schema-theoretic view of basic processes in reading comprehension. In P.D. Pearson, R. Barr, M.L. Kamil, & P. Mosenthal (Eds.), *Handbook of reading research* (pp. 225–253). New York: Longman.

Au, K.H., & Raphael, T.E. (2000). Equity and literacy in the next millennium. *Reading Research Quarterly, 35*, 170–188.

August, D., & Shanahan, T. (2006). Synthesis: Instruction and professional development. In D. August & T. Shanahan (Eds.), *Developing literacy in second-language learners: Report of the National Literacy Panel on Language-Minority Children and Youth*. Mahwah, NJ: Erlbaum.

Baker, L., Afflerbach, P., & Reinking, D. (1996). Developing engaged readers in school and home communities: An overview. In L. Baker, P. Afflerbach, & D. Reinking (Eds.), *Developing engaged readers in school and home communities* (pp. xiii–xxvii). Hillsdale, NJ: Erlbaum.

Baker, L., & Wigfield, A. (1999). Dimensions of children's motivation for reading and their relations to reading activity and reading achievement. *Reading Research Quarterly, 34*, 452–477.

Barone, D.M., & Morrow, L.M. (Eds.). (2002). *Literacy and young children: Research-based practices*. New York: Guilford.

Baumann, J.F., & Kame'enui, E.J. (1991). Research on vocabulary instruction: Ode to

Flesch, R. (1955). *Why Johnny can't read*. New York: Harper & Row.

Freire, P. (1970). *Pedagogy of the oppressed*. New York: Herder and Herder.

Freire, P. (1983). The importance of the act of reading. *Journal of Education, 165*, 5–11.

Fries, C.C. (1963). *Linguistics and reading*. Austin, TX: Holt, Rinehart and Winston.

Goodman, K.S. (1965). A linguistic study of cues and miscues in reading. *Elementary English, 42*, 639–643.

Goodman, K.S. (1967). Reading: A psycholinguistic guessing game. *Journal of the Reading Specialist, 6*, 126–135.

Guthrie, J. (Ed.). (1981). *Comprehension and teaching: Research reviews*. Newark, DE: International Reading Association.

Guthrie, J.T., & Alvermann, D. (Eds.). (1999). *Engagement in reading: Processes, practices, and policy implications*. New York: Teachers College Press.

Guthrie, J.T., & Wigfield, A. (1997). *Reading engagement: Motivating readers through integrated curriculum*. Newark, DE: International Reading Association.

Hamm, D., & Pearson, P.D. (2002). Reading-comprehension processes. In B.J. Guzzetti (Ed.), *Literacy in America: An encyclopedia of history, theory, and practice* (Vol. 2, pp. 508–515). Santa Barbara, CA: ABC-CLIO.

Harris, T.L., & Hodges, R.E. (Eds.). (1995). *The literacy dictionary: The vocabulary of reading and writing*. Newark, DE: International Reading Association.

Harvey, S., & Goudvis, A. (2000). *Strategies that work: Teaching comprehension to enhance understanding*. Portland, ME: Stenhouse.

Hilden, K., & Pressley, M. (2002). *Can teachers become comprehension strategy teachers given a small amount of training?* Paper presented at the 52nd annual meeting of the National Reading Conference, Miami, FL.

Hoffman, J., & Pearson, P.D. (2000). Reading teacher education in the next millennium: What your grandmother's teacher didn't know that your granddaughter's teacher should. *Reading Research Quarterly, 35*, 28–44.

Holmes, J.A. (1953). *The substrata-factor theory of reading*. Berkeley, CA: California Book Co.

International Reading Association. (2002). *Evidence-based reading instruction: Putting the National Reading Panel report into practice*. Newark, DE: Author.

Kintsch, W. (1974). *The representation of meaning in memory*. Hillsdale, NJ: Erlbaum.

Kintsch, W. (2004). The construction–integration model of text comprehension and its implications for instruction. In R.B. Ruddell & N.J. Unrau (Eds.), *Theoretical models and processes of reading* (5th ed., pp. 1270–1328). Newark, DE: International Reading Association.

LaBerge, D., & Samuels, S.J. (1976). Toward a theory of automatic information processing in reading. In H. Singer & R.B. Ruddell (Eds.), *Theoretical models and processes of reading* (2nd ed., pp. 548–579). Newark, DE: International Reading Association.

Leu, D.J. (2002). Literacy and technology: Deictic consequences for literacy education in an information age. In M.L. Kamil, P. Mosenthal, P.D. Pearson, & R. Barr (Eds.), *Handbook of reading research* (Vol. 3, pp. 743–770). Mahwah, NJ: Erlbaum.

Leu, D.J., & Kinzer, C.K. (2000). The convergence of literacy instruction with networked technologies for information and communication. *Reading Research Quarterly, 35*, 108–127.

Luke, A., & Freebody, P. (1999). Further notes on the four resources model. *Reading Online*. Retrieved May 4, 2007, from www.readingonline.org/research/lukefreebody.html

Mathewson, G.C. (2004). Model of attitude influence upon reading and learning to read. In R.B. Ruddell & N.J. Unrau (Eds.), *Theoretical models and processes of reading* (5th ed., pp. 1431–1461). Newark, DE: International Reading Association.

McLaughlin, M. (2003). *Guided comprehension in the primary grades: A framework for curricularizing strategy instruction*. Paper presented at the 53rd annual meeting of the National Reading Conference, Scottsdale, AZ.

McLaughlin, M., & Allen, M.B. (2002). *Guided comprehension: A teaching model for grades 3–8*. Newark, DE: International Reading Association.

McLaughlin, M., & DeVoogd, G. (2004). Critical literacy as comprehension: Expanding reader response. *Journal of Adolescent & Adult Literacy, 48*, 52–62.

Morrow, L.M. (2000). *Literacy development in the early years: Helping children read and write* (4th ed.). Boston: Allyn & Bacon.

National Commission on Teaching and America's Future. (1997). *Doing what matters most: Investing in quality teaching*. Retrieved October 15, 2007, from www.tcrecord.org/pdf/10417.pdf

National Institute of Child Health and Human Development. (2000). *Report of the National Reading Panel. Teaching children to read: An evidence-based assessment of the scientific*

Ruddell, R.B. (1995). Those influential reading teachers: Meaning negotiators and motivation builders. *The Reading Teacher, 48*, 454–463.

Ruddell, R.B., & Unrau, N.J. (2004a). Reading as a meaning-construction process: The reader, the text, and the teacher. In R.B. Ruddell & N.J. Unrau (Eds.), *Theoretical models and processes of reading* (5th ed., pp. 1462–1521). Newark, DE: International Reading Association.

Ruddell, R.B., & Unrau, N.J. (Eds.). (2004b). *Theoretical models and processes of reading* (5th ed.). Newark, DE: International Reading Association.

Rumelhart, D.E. (1975). Notes on a schema for stories. In D.G. Bobrow & A.M. Collins (Eds.), *Representation and understanding: Studies in cognitive psychology* (pp. 211–236). New York: Academic.

Rumelhart, D.E. (2004). Toward an interactive model of reading. In R.B. Ruddell & N.J. Unrau (Eds.), *Theoretical models and processes of reading* (5th ed., pp. 864–894). Newark, DE: International Reading Association.

Sadoski, M. (1999). Comprehending comprehension. *Reading Research Quarterly, 34*, 493–500.

Sadoski, M., & Paivio, A. (2004). A dual coding theoretical model of reading. In R.B. Ruddell & N.J. Unrau (Eds.), *Theoretical models and processes of reading* (5th ed., pp. 1329–1362). Newark, DE: International Reading Association.

Samuels, S.J. (2004). Theory of automatic information processing in reading revisited. information processing in reading In R.B. Ruddell & N.J. Unrau (Eds.), *Theoretical mod-els and processes of reading* (5th ed., pp. 1127–1148). Newark, DE: International Reading Association.

Singer, H. (1985). A century of landmarks in reading research. In H. Singer & R.B. Ruddell (Eds.), *Theoretical models and processes of reading* (3rd ed., pp. 8–20). Newark, DE: International Reading Association.

Smith, F. (1971). *Understanding reading: A psycholinguistic analysis of reading and learning to read.* Austin, TX: Holt, Rinehart and Winston.

Snow, C.E., Burns, M.S., & Griffin, P.G. (Eds.). (1998). *Preventing reading difficulties in young children.* Washington, DC: National Academy Press.

Stahl, S.A., Duffy-Hester, A.M., & Stahl, K.A.D. (1998). Theory and research in practice: Everything you wanted to know about phonics (but were afraid to ask). *Reading Research Quarterly, 33*, 338–355.

Strickland, D.S. (1998). *Teaching phonics for educators: A primer for educators.* Newark, DE: International Reading Association.

Tierney, R.J. (1992). Ongoing research and new directions. In J.W. Irwin & M.A. Doyle (Eds.), *Reading/writing connections: Learning from research* (pp. 246–259). Newark, DE: International Reading Association.

Vygotsky, L.S. (1978). *Mind in society: The development of higher psychological processes* (M. Cole, V. John-Steiner, S. Scribner, & E. Souberman, Eds. & Trans.). Cambridge, MA: Harvard University Press. (Original work published 1934).

Wink, J. (2000). *Critical pedagogy: Notes from the real world* (2nd ed.). New York: Longman.

Schreiber (1980) noted that grouping words into syntactically appropriate phrases while reading was essential to comprehension. And then Allington (1983) challenged reading scholars and practitioners to consider reading fluency, in its various conceptions, an important—but up to that point neglected—goal of effective reading instruction. It was at that point that I thought that there was something to this thing called fluency and that it was worth pursuing in my doctoral dissertation and beyond.

Maryann Mraz

As a doctoral student at Kent State University, I was affected by Tim's work in the area of fluency. In one of his reading seminar courses, I recalled my own experiences as an elementary school student: A textbook would be opened to a brand new chapter and, one by one, up and down the neatly arranged rows of desks, each student would take a turn reading aloud a paragraph from the never-before-seen pages. Like many students, I would count the number of readers and the number of paragraphs to go in order to figure out which paragraph would be mine to read to the group. Then, like many students, not wanting to sound like a poor reader in front of my classmates, I would practice reading that paragraph silently, paying no attention to its meaning or to the meaning of any of the other paragraphs, until it was my turn to read aloud in this round-robin reading ordeal.

Years later, in my work with both students and teachers, the need to implement instructional strategies that would support fluent reading and, in turn, comprehension in a more effective manner than that of the traditional strategies I recalled as a child was apparent. Also clear was the need to better understand the role of fluency in the context of reading programs, as well as what fluency strategies would be effective, under what circumstances, and for whom.

D espite its relative invisibility, reading fluency has been part of the history of scholarly inquiry in reading. In this chapter, we provide a historical perspective of the role of fluency in reading; discuss how the definition of fluency and the use of instructional strategies, such as round-robin reading and repeating reading, have changed over time; present key fluency research from the second half of the 20th century; and examine fluency today. We wrap up the chapter by posing a number of questions that may drive future research in fluency, and we provide some resources that we consider essential in studying this topic.

community life. Some researchers, such as Huey (1908), noted that, while oral reading activities were the focus of most reading instruction in schools, silent reading predominated everyday life.

During the first half of the 20th century, silent reading with an emphasis on comprehension began to replace oral reading with a focus on elocution not only as a goal for reading but as the preferred mode of reading instruction. According to Smith (2002), schools became nearly obsessed with the notion of silent reading for improving comprehension and reading speed. In fact, from the 1930s through the early 1940s, Chicago schools adopted a program called the nonoral method, which emphasized the teaching of silent reading exclusively. Followers taught students to gain meaning directly from printed symbols by using only their eyes and central nervous system, rather than by using inner speech (McDade, 1944; Rohrer, 1943).

The shift toward silent reading and away from oral reading was also supported by the beginning of the standardized testing movement in the early 20th century. Reading achievement tests were administered in a silent reading format in order to evaluate the progress of both individual students and schools. A series of school evaluation studies conducted by William S. Gray in the early 1900s showed overwhelmingly that students with higher levels of silent reading proficiency performed best on the standardized assessments (Hoffman, 1991). The historical trend of administering reading tests that lacked a specific fluency component, either oral or silent, continued from the 1920s through the 1990s.

The Rise of Round-Robin Reading

The demise of oral reading as the focus of reading instruction in the 20th century, and the emphasis on comprehension and silent reading as the primary tools for attaining high levels of reading achievement, did not lead to the disappearance of oral reading as an instructional practice. Oral reading, typically in the form of round-robin reading, continued as a mainstay of reading instruction throughout the second half of the 20th century (Austin & Morrison, 1963; Optiz & Rasinski, 1998). When round-robin reading, the teacher typically called on students one by one to read orally a passage the student had neither seen previously nor rehearsed. Students were assessed on the accuracy of their reading and may have been given instruction in the words they missed or on any word patterns with which they experienced difficulty reading.

Round-robin reading was usually done as whole-class instruction, and it offered the teacher advantages beyond assessing students' oral reading. It gave the

of inside-the-head topics, such as comprehension, was discouraged during be-haviorism" (p. 13).

With the advent of the new paradigm of cognitive psychology in the mid-1960s, research on comprehension and fluency began to emerge. Support for investigating these "inside-the-head" topics came, in part, from the development of psycholinguistics, the area of language inquiry that combines a psychologi-cal understanding of the reading process with an understanding of how lan-guage works (Vacca et al., 2006). Psycholinguistics purports that reading is neither a passive nor an exact process. Rather, it is an active thinking process in which all readers make use of what Goodman (1973) termed *cueing systems* (see also chapters 1, 2, 5, 8, 9, and 10, this volume, for more on Goodman's contributions).

In their seminal volume on reading, Gibson and Levin (1975) discuss oral reading, expressive reading, and reading rate, but they stop short of connect-ing these aspects of reading to one's overall reading proficiency. Since the early 1970s, significant advances in our understandings of reading have prompted scholars to reexamine reading fluency.

Automaticity Theory

One of the more important milestones in contemporary conceptions of reading fluency came with the publication of Laberge and Samuels's (1974) theory of automatic information process in reading. This was perhaps the first modern theoretical conception of reading fluency. Laberge and Samuels argued that the surface-level processing of words in reading (e.g., visual perception, sounds, phrasing words together) should ideally be done at an automatic level, a level that required minimal attention or cognitive capacity. In doing so, readers could reserve their finite cognitive resources for the more important task in reading—comprehension. For many readers, it could be hypothesized, poor comprehension or difficulty in comprehension could be explained by readers needing to invest too much of their cognitive resources in the surface-level aspects of reading—slow, laborious, conscious-filled decoding of words. This investment of cognitive resources into the surface-level com-ponent of reading depleted or exhausted what could be invested in making sense of what they read.

Samuels (1979) hypothesized that automaticity finds its way into many human activities. For example, athletes and musicians have developed skills within their repertoire to a level at which they perform seemingly without effort—automatically. First, they work with a teacher or coach who helps them

The Influence of the National Reading Panel

In 1997, the National Institute of Child Health and Human Development (NICHD) was charged to convene a National Reading Panel (NRP), a panel of experts who would assess the status of research-based knowledge of reading and the effectiveness of instructional methods used to teach children to read. The NRP built upon the earlier work of the National Research Council published in *Preventing Reading Difficulties in Young Children* (Snow, Burns, & Griffin, 1998).

In the past decade, the policy document *The Report of the National Reading Panel* (NICHD, 2000) raised awareness of the important role fluency plays in overall reading development. The NRP report identified the most important research-based factors associated with high achievement in learning to read in the elementary grades. It identified reading fluency as one of five key instructional areas critical to producing proficient readers. The finding that certain instructional practices, such as guided oral reading, promote reading development throughout the elementary grades has helped educators to consider fundamental changes in the use of oral reading instruction in the reading program.

Today, with the advancement of research, fluency is recognized as a multidimensional concept (Kuhn & Stahl, 2000). Padak and Rasinski (in press) define fluency as a bridge that connects decoding to comprehension. This bridge consists of three support structures: accuracy, automaticity, and prosody. Accurate decoding is an essential part of fluent reading. If a reader is unable to decode the words he or she sees in print, then reading cannot occur. Accurate decoding, however, is not enough. Fluent reading requires automatic decoding on the part of readers.

Automaticity theory explains how people become adept at performing complex and difficult tasks. In order to read fluently, readers need to recognize words automatically so they can use their cognitive resources for constructing meaning rather than on decoding words. When, for example, a student has had ample opportunities to practice reading high-frequency words that appear in a text, these words can be decoded with ease, speed, and accuracy. Because the decoding task has required minimal amounts of the student's cognitive capacity, more of the student's resources can be directed toward understanding the text.

Prosodic reading, or prosody, the third support of the fluency bridge, refers to the ability of a reader to chunk the text into syntactically and semantically appropriate units and to interpret the text by reading with appropriate expression (Schreiber, 1991). When a reader reads expressively with appropriate phras-

- What is the incidence of reading fluency difficulties at various ages and grade levels?
- How should fluency be assessed? Do current assessment practices rely too heavily on reading rate? How can prosodic reading be effectively assessed?
- How can we help teachers and parents to understand the link between fluent reading and reading comprehension?
- What role can technology play in teaching and assessing reading fluency in students?

Final Thoughts

Fluency is an important part of the reading process, and it should be part of any effective reading curriculum. The potential for better understanding fluency, and in doing so improving students' overall achievement in reading, is strong. The Essential Readings on Fluency will provide you with resources to deepen your study and understanding of fluency and the role it plays in overall reading proficiency. Let us hope that the past is not prologue for the reading future—that fluency does not once again become relegated to the neglected goal of the reading curriculum and that reading fluency remains a significant variable for theory building, research, and instruction in reading.

ESSENTIAL READINGS ON FLUENCY

Allington, R.L. (1983). Fluency: The neglected reading goal. *The Reading Teacher, 36*, 556–561.

Elderedge, J.L., & Butterfield, D. (1986). Alternatives to traditional reading instruction. *The Reading Teacher, 40*, 32–37.

Kuhn, M.R., & Stahl, S.A. (2000). *Fluency: A review of developmental and remedial practices*. Ann Arbor, MI: Center for the Improvement of Early Reading Achievement.

Rasinski, T.V. (1989). Fluency for everyone: Incorporating fluency instruction in the classroom. *The Reading Teacher, 42*, 690–693.

Rasinski, T.V. (2003). *The fluent reader: Oral reading strategies for building word recognition, fluency, and comprehension*. New York: Scholastic.

Rasinski, T.V., Blachowicz, C., & Lems, K. (2006). *Fluency instruction: Research-based best practices*. New York: Guilford.

Rasinski, T.V., & Hoffman, J.V. (2003). Oral reading in the school literacy curriculum. *Reading Research Quarterly, 38*, 510–522.

marching off to Vietnam. I cried at my failure but had no clue what I might have done differently. The title of an article I wrote about Larry and me much later was "Atoning for My Sins or What I Would Do If I Could Do It Over" (Richardson, 1980). Essentially, I have spent the rest of my career trying to "do it over" through content area reading.

Two years later, I arrived on Okinawa, where I lived for three years during the Vietnam War. I used my meager experience to teach men in the Armed Forces who had not met the literacy requirements; the need for soldiers in Vietnam called for the relaxation of literacy standards. I provided on-the-spot literacy skill instruction before these young men were sent to fight. As with Larry, I wanted to help, but I had limited understanding of how to do so.

Three years and two children later, I went back to graduate school. I chose education and the area of reading instead of English literature. My heart is always with my content area, but I had enough experience by then to realize that what I could contribute best in the world was effective literacy instruction for students in my subject matter.

I have always thought like a content area teacher, and I act out of that thought, constantly trying to apply my knowledge in effective reading-based ways so that I can reach the Larrys I meet. I apply Abraham Maslow's (1966) quote: "If the only tool you have is a hammer, you tend to treat everything as if it were a nail" (pp. 15–16). I look for lots of tools now and see much more than nails in content area reading.

My purpose for this chapter is not to replicate scholarly reviews of research such as the history of content area reading conducted by Moore, Readence, and Rickelman (1983) or the history of comprehension conducted by Robinson, Faraone, Hittleman, and Unruh (1990). The choices of articles and citations within this chapter are my own and do not represent the entire body of work pertaining to content area reading from 1956–2006. They are meant to be representative and illustrative rather than exhaustive and inclusive.

I have limited my scope to the K–12 sector. I do not comment about vocabulary and comprehension studies unless they have had a specific impact on content area reading, because these topics are covered in other chapters of the book. My qualifying question (admittedly subjective) was, Did this resource make a difference in how we view content area reading today? My goals were to present

- Children should learn to read "real literature," e.g., books, papers, records, letters, children's own experiences or thoughts. These should be read as the need arises in a child's life.

- Study skills such as library skills and note-taking should be taught as early as possible in the elementary grades.

- In high school, students should be given free rein to read widely on subjects of interest. This is preferable to a focused and analytical study of a few texts and authors.

- Real reading should increase rather than decrease in importance among school studies. (Huey, 1908/1968, pp. 6–7)

Gray (1919), Gates (1935), and McKee (1934) all advocated for "separate instruction in content area reading skills during reading lessons with provisions for later opportunities for transfer to content areas" (Moore et al., 1983, p. 426). A key theme in the 36th NSSE Yearbook (Whipple, 1937) was that every teacher should be a teacher of reading. This idea has been appropriated by many experts in the field of content area reading to encourage the practice of reading to learn by all teachers—especially content area teachers. For instance, Gray, who contributed a chapter in Whipple's 36th Yearbook, emphasized in his writing over several years the responsibility of all teachers in content subjects, and he felt it was important to pay attention to study and training in different subjects (Guthrie, 1984).

Strang published several texts and articles in the 1920s through the 1960s about improving reading and study in high school, such as "The Improvement of Reading in High School" (Strang, 1937) and "Progress in the Teaching of Reading in High School and College" (1962). Her audience was the secondary teacher and student. Artley (1943) and Aukerman (1948) also addressed the relevance of reading for the secondary student. Robinson's (1946) introduction of the study strategy SQ3R (Survey the material, create Questions to guide their reading, then Read, Reflect, and Recite) is historically important to content area reading, because it was designed to put readers in charge of their own study of content material. This strategic activity was quite popular with teachers (although not so popular with students, because—at least in my own case—it required a specific set of steps that seemed restrictive to them). Robinson (1978) led the way to other similar study strategies that were special to content area reading, such as PQ4R (Preview, Question, Read, Reflect, Recite, Review), and SRR (Survey, Read, Review). In the 1920s through 1950s, content area reading moved to both a secondary and an activities-based emphasis.

in a few years of one another indicated that students experience difficulty with higher-level reading and writing skills such as critical thinking, drawing inferences, and applying what is read. Applebee, Langer, and Mullis (1987) maintained in *Learning to Be Literate in America* that students were having difficulty because schools were not teaching students to learn how to learn.

A Nation at Risk (Gardner et al., 1983) demonstrated the concerns for a more reading-to-learn approach, as the following quotes indicate:

> Learning is the indispensable investment required for success in the "information age" we are entering. (excerpt from section "The Risk," n.p.)

> Average achievement of high school students on most standardized tests is now lower than 26 years ago when Sputnik was launched. (excerpt from section "Indicators of the Risk," n.p.)

In response, in *Becoming a Nation of Readers*, Anderson, Hiebert, Scott, and Wilkinson (1985; see also chapters 2, 4, and 8, this volume, for discussion of this publication) gave the following recommendations:

- Teachers should devote more time to comprehension instruction.
- Textbooks should contain adequate explanations of important concepts.
- Schools should maintain well-stocked and managed libraries. (pp. 118–119)

What Works: Research About Teaching and Learning (U.S. Department of Education, 1987), advocated devoting more attention to study skills, reading to learn in specific disciplines, and using prior knowledge to learn new content. The "Education Summit" of 1989 led to *Goals 2000* (Austin, n.d.). Goal three is especially relevant to content area reading:

> American students will leave grades 4, 8, and 12 having demonstrated competency over challenging subject matter including English, mathematics, science, foreign languages, civics and government, economics, art, history, and geography; and every school in America will ensure that all students learn to use their minds well, so they may be prepared for responsible citizenship, further learning, and productive employment in our nation's modern economy. (n.p.)

Several themes emerged in the late 1980s. First, there was emphasis on strategies and activities specifically tailored for content area reading and reading to learn. The most pivotal article, in my estimation, is Donna Ogle's "K-W-L: A Teaching Model That Develops Active Reading of Expository Text" (1986). After Ogle's article, content area reading activities could be found in many articles in reading journals. For instance, Palincsar and Brown (1986) presented reciprocal reading as a way to promote independent reading from text in *The Reading*

not defined by courses of study or suggested programs, but by one particular artifact, the grade-level-specific text" (p. 85).

A multitext viewpoint was one solution. Content area reading did not have to be about one textbook per content area; many texts or varying levels could better meet the needs of students in content classrooms. Using a variety of resources, including newspapers, magazines, novels, and other informational texts beyond the textbook, became a trend. Calfee (1987) noted that trade books offer causal relationships between concepts and provide a better framework for students to answer their own questions as they read. Hughes (1987) explained how to find supplemental resources. Other means than readability formulas were shared as ways to locate resources on many reading levels (Danielson, 1987), even as Fry (1989) continued to stress the value of the Fry readability formula as a way to locate appropriately leveled text resources.

The fourth theme of the 1980s was to embrace once more the elementary as well as the secondary emphasis of content area reading (remember Gray and Huey in the early 1900s?). It is interesting to note that Ogle (1986) and Palincsar and Brown (1986) published in *The Reading Teacher*, a journal for grades K–8, but most articles about strategies and activities had been published in the *Journal of Adolescent & Adult Literacy* and other secondary-based journals, showing the continuing emphasis on content area reading as more relevant to secondary teachers. By contrast—and repeating history—Gauthier (1989) and Cudd and Roberts (1989) made the case for reading and writing in content materials in *The Reading Teacher*. In 1990, Richardson and Morgan reintroduced the K–12 emphasis of content area reading in their methods textbook. They maintained that it was time to "go back" to the roots of content area reading and embrace reading to learn for all students.

The 1990s: Strategic Reading

Political and social influences continued to have an impact on content area reading in the 1990s, and one can derive several themes for this decade. First, a continuing theme was comparison to other countries in academics. In *How in the World Do Children Read?* Elley (1992) reiterated the competition that the United States faced in producing good readers who can contribute to their society. In the countries with the highest rates of literacy, wide reading in many subjects was found to be a crucial factor.

Second, as in the 1980s, there was an emphasis on strategies and activities specifically tailored for content area reading and reading to learn. Alvermann, O'Brien, and Dillon (1990) looked at teachers' instruction and

content (Alvermann et al., 1996). When students could select their own learning strategies, they felt successful as learners (Quiocho, 1997) and could address their own issues about text (Lester & Cheek, 1998).

The fourth theme, new respect for the use of many resources at many levels, was gaining ground. The *Journal of Adolescent & Adult Literacy* published a column about using literature to spark interest in subject matter (Richardson, 1994–1998). By looking at student perceptions of content area reading, we realized that students do not lose interest in their content, but they lose interest in the textbooks as their main resource (Bintz, 1993). Fry's (1990) proposed readability formula for short passages may have encouraged teachers to look beyond the textbook to shorter and more interesting material. Stahl, Hynd, Britton, McNish, and Bosquet (1996) cautioned that students need specific instruction in the use of multiple resources and helpful notes to broaden their perspectives when studying from multiple sources in history. The term *new literacies* (Alexander, Kulikowich, & Jetton, 1994) was introduced to emphasize media other than the book as important sources for gaining content knowledge. (See also Chapter 8, this volume, for further discussion of new literacies.)

Fifth, the importance of background knowledge in reading was highlighted. Researchers (Reynolds, Sinatra, & Jetton, 1996) placed a strong emphasis on the social construction of knowledge and the idea that students have to pull from shared knowledge to complete a task. To solve problems, professionals noted that students with considerable background knowledge of the subject are able to use strategies more effectively than those with little background knowledge (Alexander & Judy, 1988). Learners with high background knowledge focus on what is important in the learning task, while those with inadequate background knowledge often search in a frantic mode, because they cannot distinguish relevant material from irrelevant material (McDonald & Stevenson, 1998). Last, O'Donnell and Kelly (1998) showed that students with low background knowledge of a topic are unable to formulate goals adequately.

Sixth, schema theory, popularized by Rumelhart (1980), offered a way of explaining how prior knowledge is stored in memory. The information a learner acquires about a topic is organized cognitively into a framework, or schema. The framework grows to include other topics, thus creating larger and larger schemata, arranged in a hierarchy. Learners retrieve information by understanding how newly encountered material links to what they already have organized cognitively. Interrelationships among schemata aid understanding (see also

Into the 21st Century: Standards-Based Learning

As in each decade from the 1950s, perceived competition with other countries for the "best" level of academic success has continued to influence this decade. Standards that could be applied across the United States became the cause célèbre. The advent of No Child Left Behind (NCLB) Act of 2001 once again politicized the field of reading, content area reading not withstanding (see also chapters 2, 3, 9, and 11, this volume, for further discussion of NCLB). The legislation called for increased attention to achievement tests at grades 3–8, and to standards for student "success." The impact on content knowledge at elementary and secondary levels has generated much discussion and concern (Conley & Hinchman, 2004). As a result of NCLB and standards-based assessment, the learner has to show competence, and teachers are evaluated on the test scores of their students. Many educators have felt that content subjects were reduced to facts and details at the expense of exploration and wide reading in the content areas. Time for deep study has dwindled due to lack of time after the test content was covered. This skills-centered instruction stifled higher order thinking and exploration, according to many educators. At the time of this writing, a movement by states to demand a more student-centered than test-centered curriculum is again on the rise. Recent articles have concentrated on the use of strategies and activities to enhance test performance (Kozen, Murray, & Windell, 2006; Raphael & Au, 2005).

Even in a time when it would seem that skills-centered instruction is predominant, great strides are being made in how we look at the learner's role in content area reading. *Constructivism* is a term used by psychologists and reading experts of this era to explain what happens as a reader processes text. Applefield, Huber, and Moallem (2000) stated,

> The field of education has undergone a significant shift in thinking about the nature of human learning and the conditions that best promote the varied dimensions of human learning. As in psychology, there has been a paradigm shift in designed instruction: from behaviorism to cognitivism and now to constructivism. (p. 36)

Constructivism may be one of the most influential views of learning during the last two decades. It is a significant learning theory that emphasizes a student-centered approach to learning. In a constructivist model, learners are building information from teacher guidance. The reader must actively construct meaning by relating new material to the known, using reasoning and developing concepts (see also chapters 1, 2, 5, 8, and 10, this volume, for more discussion of constructivism).

many activities and strategies in content area reading (Barry, 2002). Some take the challenge seriously enough to devise curriculum responsive to all of their students (Brozo & Hargis, 2003). Some teachers pair up across content areas to promote better content area reading instruction (Donahue, 2003; Howes, Hamilton, & Zaskoda, 2003). Student attitudes continue to fluctuate (Richardson, 2000), dependent on their interest in subject matter and on the teacher's ability to engage them in learning.

> Teachers' attitudes are changing toward a more positive stance about content area reading, especially as they see themselves as readers and learners in content area reading.

The "the age of multiliteracies" (Turbill, 2002), when one reads text plus "color, sound, movement, and visual representations" (n.p.), became a predominant consideration in the early 2000s. Some call this the *new literacies* (Kist, 2000; Leu, Kinzer, Coiro, & Cammack, 2004; Moje, Labbo, Baumann, & Gaskins, 2000; Moje et al., 2004). Although the actual literacy skills required in the technological age are not new, the *way* in which electronic materials must be read is new. As Reinking (1997) noted, although technology itself is neutral, the way we use it to learn enables learners to be more creative and engaged. A reader still must use comprehension, vocabulary, and study skills to construct meaning, but the behaviors that students must use are different than those required for a paper-based environment. For instance, when reading from a textbook, one may write notes on index cards or sticky notes. When reading on a computer, one may take notes by inserting remarks into the document with red font, or even by using track editing or footnoting. The age of multiliteracies is helping to reintroduce study skills—an area dormant since the early 1900s—into content area reading. Readers must now be information literate (Henderson & Scheffler, 2004), that is, able to find and use information in any form, including paper or electronic forms (see also Chapter 8, this volume, for further discussion of new literacies).

Out of new literacies research has come a plethora of new activities that were not even possible before the 1980s. Students can use chat rooms (Albright, Purohit, & Walsh, 2002) to discuss their learning; they map online (Love, 2002); they use online discussions to discuss content (Thomas & Hofmeister, 2003). WebQuests and Treasure Hunts are now designed by content teachers to guide their students on the Internet to content information that is informative and suitable. Hypertext enables students to create their own quick references to word meanings, and outlining software facilitates study. As the next section on the 21st century illustrates, the impact of technology on content reading is an ever-expanding area of study.

- How do we ensure that teachers and students remain positive about content area reading?
- How will the reader who relies more and more on electronic text evolve and grow in content area reading?

Final Thoughts

We need to improve on the past instead of repeating it; in order to accomplish this, we should read the works of past scholars and note how these works can influence today's research and practice. When we look for themes and follow them across time, we can see what changes the interest and focus from time to time and use this information to capitalize on and expand as well as introduce new ideas (without neglecting past contributions). I have included a list of some Essential Readings on Content Area Reading to serve as a starting point for the aspiring researcher.

We must realize that there is no quick fix, nor is there one magic content area reading activity! One must be mindful of the strategic aspect of reading and the place of activities in aiding readers to learn. Researchers and scholars should follow where they are most interested and use what they learn to broaden their scope. That is the nature of content area reading—so much branches to so much else.

Finally, we must realize that political interests will influence historical trends and find ways to be proactive before being forced to be reactive.

ESSENTIAL READINGS ON CONTENT AREA READING

Armbruster, B.B., Echols, C.H., & Brown, A.L. (1983). *The role of metacognition in reading to learn: A developmental perspective.* Champaign, IL: University of Illinois, Center for the Study of Reading.

Brown A.L., Campione, J.C., & Day J.D. (1981). Learning to learn: On training students to learn from texts. *Educational Researcher, 10,* 2, 14–21.

Gray, W.S. (1984). *Reading: A research retrospective, 1881–1941.* (J.T. Guthrie, Ed.). Newark: DE: International Reading Association.

Hynd, C. (1999). Teaching students to think critically using multiple texts in history. *Journal of Adolescent & Adult Literacy, 42,* 428–436.

Matthews, M.M. (1966). *Teaching to read, historically considered.* Chicago: University of Chicago Press.

Austin, T.L. (n.d.). *Goals 2000—The Clinton administration education program*. Retrieved October 12, 2006, from www.nd.edu/~rbarger/www7/goals200.html

Barry, A.L. (2002). Reading strategies teachers say they use. *Journal of Adolescent & Adult Literacy, 46*, 132–141.

Bean, T.W. (1997). Preservice teachers' selection and use of content area literacy strategies. *Journal of Educational Research, 90*, 154–163.

Bean, T.W., & Ericson, B.O. (1989). Text previews and three level study guides for content area critical reading. *Journal of Reading, 32*, 337–341.

Beck, I.L., & McKeown, M.G. (1988). Toward meaningful accounts in history texts for young learners. *Educational Researcher, 17*, 31–39.

Bintz, W.P. (1993). Resistant readers in secondary education: Some insights and implications. *Journal of Reading, 36*, 604–615.

Bintz, W.P. (1997). Exploring reading nightmares of middle and secondary school teachers. *Journal of Adolescent & Adult Literacy, 41*, 12–24.

Blachowicz, C.L., & Obrochta, C. (2005). Vocabulary visits: Virtual field trips for content vocabulary development. *The Reading Teacher, 59*, 262–268.

Bloom, A.D. (1987). *The closing of the American mind*. New York: Simon & Schuster.

Bragstad, M.B. (1975). Teaching students how to learn. *Journal of Reading, 19*, 226–230.

Brown A.L., Campione, J.C., & Day J.D. (1981). Learning to learn: On training students to learn from texts. *Educational Researcher, 10*, 2, 14–21.

Brozo, W.G. (1988). Applying a reader response heuristic to expository text. *Journal of Reading, 32*, 140–145.

Brozo, W.G., & Hargis, C.H. (2003). Taking seriously the idea of reform: One high school's efforts to make reading more responsive to all students. *Journal of Adolescent & Adult Literacy, 47*, 14–23.

Bryant, J.E.P. (1971). *An investigation of the reading levels of high school students with the readability levels of certain content textbooks with their costs*. Dissertation, The Florida State University. (ERIC Document Reproduction Service No. ED072411)

Buehl, D. (1998). Integrating the "R" word into the high school curriculum: Developing reading programs for adolescent learners. *NASSP Bulletin, 82*, 57–66.

Bulgren, J., & Scanlon, D. (1997/1998). Instructional routines and learning strategies that promote understanding of content area concepts. *Journal of Adolescent & Adult Literacy, 41*, 292–302.

Burmeister, L.E. (1978). *Reading strategies for middle and secondary school teachers* (2nd ed.). Reading, MA: Addison-Wesley Higher Education.

Calfee, R.C. (1987). *The role of text structure in acquiring knowledge: Final report to the U.S. Department of Education* (Federal Program No. 122B). Palo Alto, CA: Stanford University, Text Analysis Project.

Carter, C.J., & Klotz, J. (1991). What every principal should know about content area reading. *NASSP Bulletin, 75*, 97–105.

Chamot, A.U., & O'Malley, J.M. (1994). Instructional approaches and teaching procedures. In K. Spangenberg-Urbschat & R. Pritchard (Eds.), *Kids come in all languages: Reading instruction for ESL students* (pp. 82–107). Newark, DE: International Reading Association.

Chapple, L., & Curtis, A. (2000). Content-based instruction in Hong Kong: Student responses to film. *System, 28*, 419–433.

Come Romine, B.G., McKenna, M.C., & Robinson, R.D. (1996). Reading coursework requirements for middle and high school content area teachers: A U.S. survey. *Journal of Adolescent & Adult Literacy, 40*, 194–198.

Conley, M.W., & Hinchman, K.A. (2004). No Child Left Behind: What it means for U.S. adolescents and what we can do about it. *Journal of Adolescent & Adult Literacy, 48*, 42–50.

Cudd, E.T., & Roberts, L. (1989). Using writing to enhance content area learning in the primary grades. *The Reading Teacher, 42*, 392–404.

Daisey, P. (1997). Promoting literacy in secondary content area classrooms with biography projects. *Journal of Adolescent & Adult Literacy, 40*, 270–278.

Daisey, P., & Shroyer, M.G. (1993). Perceptions and attitudes of content and methods instructors toward a required reading course. *Journal of Reading, 36*, 624–629.

Danielson, K.E. (1987). Readability formulas: A necessary evil? *Reading Horizons, 27*, 178–188.

D'Arcangelo, M. (2002). The challenge of content-area reading. A conversation with Donna Ogle. *Educational Leadership, 60*, 12–15.

Davey, B. (1988). How do classroom teachers use their textbooks? *Journal of Reading, 31*, 340–345.

Dechant, E.V. (1970). *Improving the teaching of reading*. Upper Saddle River, NJ: Prentice Hall.

Donahue, D.M. (2000). Experimenting with texts: New science teachers' experience and

Howes, E.V., Hamilton, G.W., & Zaskoda, D. (2003). Linking science and literature through technology: Thinking about interdisciplinary inquiry in middle school. *Journal of Adolescent & Adult Literacy, 46*, 494–504.

Huey, E.B. (1968). *The psychology and pedagogy of reading.* Cambridge, MA: MIT Press. (Original work published 1908)

Hughes, S. (1987). Finding good literature to supplement content area instruction: bibliographic sources. *The Reading Teacher, 40*, 568–570.

Hynd, C. (1999). Teaching students to think critically using multiple texts in history. *Journal of Adolescent & Adult Literacy, 42*, 428–436.

Jetton, T.L., & Alexander, P.A. (1997). Instructional importance: What teachers value and what students learn. *Reading Research Quarterly, 32*, 290–308.

Keenan, D.M. (1976). *A study of the relationship between tenth grade students' reading ability and their comprehension of certain assigned textbooks.* Unpublished doctoral dissertation, Florida State University.

Kirsch, I.S., Jungeblut, A., Johnson, E., & Educational Testing Service. (1986). *Literacy: Profiles of America's young adults: Final report.* Princeton, NJ: National Assessment of Educational Progress.

Kist, W. (2000). Beginning to create the new literacy classroom: What does the new literacy look like? *Journal of Adolescent & Adult Literacy, 43*, 710–718.

Kozen, A.A., Murray, R.K., & Windell, I. (2006). Increasing all students' chance to achieve: Using and adapting anticipation guides with middle school learners. *Intervention in School and Clinic, 41*, 195–200.

Last, D., O'Donnell, A.M., & Kelly, A.E. (1998, March). *Using hypermedia: Effects of prior knowledge and goal strength.* Paper presented at the annual meeting of the Society for Information Technology in Teacher Education international conference, Washington, DC.

Lester, J.H., & Cheek, E.H.(1998). The "real" experts address the textbook issues. *Journal of Adolescent & Adult Literacy, 41*, 282–291.

Leu, D.J., Jr., Kinzer, C.K., Coiro, J.L., & Cammack, D.W. (2004). Toward a theory of new literacies emerging from the Internet and other communication technologies. In R. Ruddell & N. Unrau (Eds.), *Theoretical models and processes of reading* (5th ed., pp. 1570–1613). Newark, DE: International Reading Association.

Love, A.M. (1991). Process and product in geology: An investigation of some discourse features of two introductory textbooks. *English for Specific Purposes, 10*(2), 89–109.

Love, K. (2002). Mapping online discussion in senior English. *Journal of Adolescent & Adult Literacy, 45*, 382–396.

Maslow, A. H. (1966). *The psychology of science: A reconnaissance.* New York: Harper & Row.

Mathison, C. (1989). Activating student interest in content area reading. *Journal of Reading, 33*, 170–176.

McAloon, N.M. (1993). Content area reading— It's not my job! *Journal of Reading, 37*, 332–334.

McDonald, S., & Stevenson, R.J. (1998). Effects of text structure and prior knowledge of the learner on navigation in hypertext. *Human Factors, 40*(1), 18–28.

McKee, P. (1934). *Reading and literature in the elementary school.* Boston: Houghton Mifflin.

Micklos, J., Jr. (1982). A look at reading achievement in the United States: The latest data. *Journal of Reading, 25*, 760–762.

Moje, E.B. (1996). "I teach students, not subjects": Teacher-student relationships as contexts for secondary literacy. *Reading Research Quarterly, 31*, 172–195.

Moje, E.B., Labbo, L.D., Baumann, J.F., & Gaskins, I.W. (2000). What will classrooms and schools look like in the new millennium? *Reading Research Quarterly, 35*, 128–134.

Moje, E.B., Ciechanowski, K.M., Kramer, K., Ellis, L., Carrillo, R., & Collazo, T. (2004). Working toward third space in content area literacy: An examination of everyday funds of knowledge and discourse. *Reading Research Quarterly, 39*, 38–70.

Moje, E.B., Young, J.P., Readence, J.E., & Moore, D.W. (2000). Reinventing adolescent literacy for new times: Perennial and millennial issues. *Journal of Adolescent & Adult Literacy, 43*, 400–410.

Moore, D.W., Bean, T.W., Birdyshaw, D., & Rycik, J.A. (1999). *Adolescent literacy: A position statement for the Commission on Adolescent Literacy of the International Reading Association.* Newark, DE: International Reading Association.

Moore, D.W., Readence, J.E., & Rickelman, R.J. (1983). An historical exploration of content area reading instruction. *Reading Research Quarterly, 18*, 419–438.

Morrow, L.M., Pressley, M., Smith, J.K., & Smith, M. (1997). The effect of a literature-based program integrated into literacy and science instruction with children from diverse backgrounds. *Reading Research Quarterly, 32*, 54–76.

Moss, B. (2005). Making a case and a place for effective content area literacy instruction in

Sticht, T. (2004, October 30). *Literacy teachers fight illiteracy during war time: A message for Veteran's Day 2004*. Retrieved October 10, 2006, from www.nald.ca/library/research/sticht/war/war.pdf

Strang, R. (1937). The improvement of reading in high school. *Teachers College Record, 39*, 197–206.

Strang, R. (1962). Progress in the teaching of reading in high school and college. *The Reading Teacher, 16*, 170–177.

Street, C. (2005). Tech talk for social studies teachers: Evaluating online resources—The importance of critical reading skills in online environments. *The Social Studies, 96*, 271–273.

Tanner, M.L., & Casados, L. (1998). Promoting and studying discussions in math class. *Journal of Adolescent & Adult Literacy, 41*, 342–350.

Thomas, M., & Hofmeister, D. (2003). Moving content area literacy into the digital age: Using online discussion board interactions. *Journal of Content Area Reading, 2*, 61–80.

Thomas, M., & Thomas, J. (2005). Seven technologies to assist ELL students in content area reading. *Journal of Content Area Reading, 4*, 65–72.

Trayer, M. (1990). Applying research in reading to the foreign language classroom. *Hispania, 73*(3), 829–832.

Turbill, J. (2002). The four ages of reading philosophy and pedagogy: A framework for examining theory and practice. *Reading Online*.

Retrieved December 12, 2004, from www.readingonline.org/international/inter_index.asp?HREF=/international/turbill4/index.html

Unsworth, L. (1999). Developing critical understanding of the specialised language of school science and history texts: A functional grammatical perspective. *Journal of Adolescent and Adult Education, 42*(7), 508–521.

Vacca, R.T. (1998). Let's not marginalize adolescent literacy. *Journal of Adolescent & Adult Literacy, 41*, 604–609.

Wade, S.E., Buxton, W.M., & Kelly, M. (1999). Using think-alouds to examine reader-text interest. *Reading Research Quarterly, 34*, 194–216.

Ward, R.A. (2005). Using children's literature to inspire K–8 preservice teachers' future mathematics pedagogy. *The Reading Teacher, 59*, 132–143.

U.S. Department of Education. (1987). *What works: Research about teaching and learning* (2nd ed.). Washington, DC: Author.

Whipple, G.M. (Ed.). (1937). *The teaching of reading: Second report* (36th Yearbook of the National Society for the Study of Education, Part I). Bloomington, IN: Public School Publishing Company.

Williams, J.P., Hall, K.M., Lauer, K.D., Stafford, K.B., DeSisto, L.A., & deCani, J.S. (2005). Expository text comprehension in the primary grade classroom. *Journal of Educational Psychology, 97*, 538–550.

Charlotte Huck, still my advisor, encouraged me to take this qualitative approach for studying children's literature in action in an elementary school (Hickman, 1981). As huge as that endeavor seemed to me at the time, the full scope of children's literature and its relation to reading is much larger.

n this chapter, I use several lenses to examine the past 50 years of children's literature. First, I detail the changing attributes of the literature itself—the changing artistry—and literature's changing role in education. Next, I discuss the influence of research that explored response and expanded uses of children's literature in the classroom. Finally, I review some of the social, institutional, professional, and advocacy influences and trends that have shaped (and still do) children's literature over the years, and I offer some guiding thoughts for future research. The list of Essential Readings on Children's Literature gives an idea of the resources I feel are most important for anyone interested in this topic.

Changes in Children's Literature and Its Role in Education

The material we call children's literature is composed of many kinds of writing and visual artistry published in a variety of genres, forms, and formats. In 1950, about 1,000 new "juveniles" were published (Kiefer, Hepler, Hickman, & Huck, 2007, p. 121). By 2005, the number was close to 10,000 (Parravano, 2006). As quantities grew, production techniques changed as well. Over the years, new technologies allowed for advances such as children's paperbacks, wipe-clean covers and pages, intricate pop-ups, and the reproduction of full-color art from almost every medium imaginable.

One way to demonstrate the scope of change in the content of children's literature is to look back at titles that broke new ground at their time of publication although their novel features have come to seem commonplace. For example, there were already plenty of engaging picture books in the 1950s, but nothing quite like *The Cat in the Hat* by Dr. Seuss (1957), with its zany pictures and a carefully worded text to invite and support beginning readers. When science fiction reflected a U.S. preoccupation with the hardware of space exploration in the mid-20th century, Madeleine L'Engle's *A Wrinkle in Time* (1962) offered up a trend-setting blend of alien worlds with the traditional conventions of fantasy. With *Where the Wild Things Are*, Maurice Sendak (1963) focused

Librarians and teachers, who for decades have taken classes in children's literature as part of their training, have also come to view children's literature as a more complex field of study. However, the kinds of scholarship that are valued and the teaching methods employed in courses for each group are distinct from each other and from English literary studies (Gupta, 2005). Education draws on many disciplines, including English and psychology, to inform children's literature studies, but the major interest is in the relationship of children's literature to learning.

While there never has been clear agreement on the place of children's literature in reading instruction, there have been notable trends. This history is reviewed in a highly recommended article by Martinez and McGee (2000), as well as in many other sources. A full century ago, literature was the commonly recommended material for school reading, although the selections tended to suit a more general audience (Clark, 2003) than books of today, which often narrowly target the concerns of particular age levels. Pervasive change began in the early 1900s with the advent of reading research that implied the need for factual material, limited vocabularies, or other content restrictions. The basal textbooks written to fit such criteria caught on, took over, and held sway throughout most of the century. Although literature did not leave the classroom, it was more often used as an extra or as a reward. (One of my own clearest memories of elementary school is seemingly endless episodes of Dick and Jane contrasted with the library table, where I could read picture books if I finished my workbook pages fast enough.) Not until the 1990s, after persistent calls for literature to become the content of reading, did research (Baumann, Hoffman, Duffy-Hester, & Ro, 2000) confirm that "real books" had regained a far more prominent place in classroom instruction—at least for a little while. (See Chapter 7, this volume, for more on literature's changing role in content area instruction.)

The Influence of Research

Just as research findings had prompted the early development of basal readers, so did various kinds of research help to fuel a resurgence of interest in teaching with children's literature. One line of research has highlighted learning outcomes and the instructional potential of specific literature experiences, such as storybook read-alouds. Many of these studies originated in questions about family literacy and early learning. Heath's (1983) study of literacy activities in working class black families, working class white families, and "mainstream" (or dominant culture) families demonstrated cultural differences in comprehension and reading engagement. Rosenblatt's work was first published in 1938, but it did not have much influence among educators until the 1960s and after, when researchers like Purves and Rippere (1968), Applebee (1978), and Galda (1982) began to look closely at the way students responded, in writing and in conversation, to various kinds of literature.

Much of the research on response has been qualitative and descriptive in nature (Hickman, 1981; Sipe, 2000; Wolf & Heath, 1992) and thus has encouraged the use of children's literature, not only by documenting particular students' successes in reading and interpretation but by providing detailed information for teachers about the planning and implementation that brought those results. Looking closely at learning in its natural context almost always brings a bonus of insights about teaching. For instance, Lehr's (1988) study of young children's developing sense of theme in stories revealed the importance of how they were asked to express themselves and in what mode—through talk or art. Likewise, the study by Eeds and Peterson (1991) that focused on children discussing literature yielded helpful guidelines for teachers.

Qualitative research also highlights the affective dimensions of literature in the classroom—attitude, motivation, pleasure, and appreciation—areas in which children's books would seem to have natural advantages over many other materials. Around the turn of the 20th century, many funders followed a pronounced conservative turn in politics by giving preference to experimental design as the only appropriate scientifically based research; attention shifted from the affective benefits of literature and once again emphasized the more easily measured aspects of reading achievement and more easily generalized means of producing them. Children's books generally are not disappearing from classrooms as a result, but time to read and discuss literature has often given way to the demands of testing and specialized instruction.

Major Social, Institutional, Professional, and Political Influences and Resulting Trends

Research is just one of many factors that influence the vitality of children's literature and its place in the classroom; others reflect the social climate, institutional and professional pressures, and even advocacy by key individuals. Political movements have a major impact because of the legislation and policy shifts they can bring. For instance, the social activism and controversial stances of the 1960s affected the content of books for children. There was a sharper edge to picture books such as Fitzhugh and Scoppettone's *Bang Bang You're*

However, approaches to literacy instruction that incorporate children's literature do remain or have been adapted for use in current classrooms. Guided reading (Fountas & Pinnell, 1996) allows for skillful teaching with reading selections at a level of increasing difficulty appropriate for individual readers. Traditionally, basal textbooks attempted to meet this need through a sequence of written-to-order stories. Guided reading reverses this practice by turning to children's literature and sequencing the difficulty of large numbers of published books through a process called *leveling* (Peterson, 2001), thus giving children and teachers a much wider range of enjoyable reading material (see also Chapter 4, this volume, for extensive discussion of guided reading). Children's books also maintain a prominent place in classrooms that use some version of literature circles (Daniels, 1994) or book clubs (McMahon & Raphael, 1997) as a structure for discussion.

Sometimes it is hard to tell whether a trend is being created or being followed, as when we look at the role of professional organizations in the growth of children's literature in the classroom. Whatever the case, it is certainly true that the International Reading Association's (IRA) level of attention to children's books increased dramatically during its first 50 years. At one time, the IRA annual convention was essentially a showcase for basal reading systems. Now the convention program book for any recent year will show multiple sessions and meetings devoted to literature (including a Special Interest Group), exhibit hall space for children's book publishers with an autograph schedule for authors and illustrators, and the presentation of awards for writing and teaching children's literature. This is a significant spotlight for a topic that has not been at the forefront of research or program funding. It seems likely that the continued presence of literature reflects the personal experience and the conviction of thousands of IRA members regarding its value in the classroom.

It's also likely that such professional attention to literature is due in part to the work of some remarkable leaders who have served the Association. For example, Bernice Cullinan, a passionate advocate for children's literature, has had far-reaching influence on teaching, writing, editing, mentoring authors, and promoting children's poetry. Another key individual was Nancy Larrick, who—in and out of IRA—laid groundwork for much of the significant attention to literature that was to come. It was her publication in the 1960s of an article titled "The All-White World of Children's Books" (Larrick, 1965), not in a professional journal but in a widely read national magazine, that called significant attention to a glaring lack of children's literature with African American and other minority protagonists.

book or discussion questions provided in a special teacher's edition of a novel. On the other hand, sometimes editors are understandably reluctant to intrude in a piece of literature that is complete in its own way and should speak for itself. We might ask ourselves if we want to maintain a line between trade books and textbooks, and where that line might be. The future, no doubt, brings research questions related to the pros and cons of the increased use of nonfiction trade books to teach content (see also Chapter 7, this volume, for further discussion of literature in the content areas). Are there advantages to using trade books for content learning? Does the depth of knowledge about content change when trade books are added to or replace textbooks?

As we continue to teach literacy through literature in its various and changing forms, we should not lose sight of why it is such a valuable resource. Of course we can use literature to show how to break the code and use the conventions. But the real contribution of literature, fiction and nonfiction, is to help us learn to feel as we think—to reflect, to consider, to care, and, perhaps even, to act on our caring. Martinez and McGee (2000) used the term *deep thinking* to describe this opportunity afforded by literature, but there are many labels that might be applied. How might future researchers expand the current lines of research regarding the use of literature to engage children in conversations about social justice and citizenship?

Final Thoughts

In 1976, while many in IRA continued to emphasize the teaching of separate reading skills, the annual convention planners invited Charlotte Huck, always an eloquent proponent of the power of literature, to give a keynote address. In that speech, reprinted several years later (Huck, 1989), she described a nonfiction book she had been reading (not a children's book but an anthropological study) that made her "realize how very fragile that which we call our humanness really is" (p. 253). Then she spoke of a novel that offered hope on the same issue. Both books, she said, led her to

> ponder the meaning of life, to consider the question of what makes us human.... No one can live long enough to see all of life clear and whole. But through wide reading as well as living, we can acquire a perception of life and literature; and on this fragile green world, a tiny globe of humanity must learn cooperation or cease to exist.... We cannot afford to educate the head without the heart. (pp. 253–254)

Whatever changes the future brings in children's books and their role in classroom reading, we would do well to keep that message in mind.

Heath, S.B. (1983). *Ways with words: Language, life, and work in communities and classrooms.* New York: Cambridge University Press.

Hickman, J. (1981). A new perspective on response to literature: Research in an elementary school setting. *Research in the Teaching of English, 15,* 343–354.

Huck, C.S. (1989). No wider than the heart is wide. In J. Hickman & B.E. Cullinan (Eds.), *Children's literature in the classroom: Weaving Charlotte's Web* (pp. 252–262). Norwood, MA: Christopher-Gordon.

Huck, C.S., & Young, D.A. (1961). *Children's literature in the elementary school.* Austin, TX: Holt, Rinehart and Winston.

Kiefer, B.Z., Hepler, S.I., Hickman, J., & Huck, C.S. (2007). *Charlotte Huck's children's literature* (9th ed.). New York: McGraw-Hill.

Larrick, N. (1965). The all-white world of children's books. *Saturday Review, 48,* 84–85.

Lehr, S. (1988). The child's developing sense of theme as a response to literature. *Reading Research Quarterly, 23,* 337–357.

Martinez, M.G., & McGee, L.M. (2000). Children's literature and reading instruction: Past, present, and future. *Reading Research Quarterly, 35,* 154–169.

McMahon, S.I., & Raphael, T.E. (Eds.). (1997). *The book club connection: Literacy learning and classroom talk.* New York: Teachers College Press; Newark, DE: International Reading Association.

Meek, M., Warlow, A., & Barton, G. (1978). *The cool web: The pattern of children's reading.* New York: Atheneum.

Meyer, L.A., Wardrop, J.L., Stahl, S.A., & Linn, R.L. (1994). How entering ability and instructional settings and not the length of the school day mediate kindergartners' reading performance. *Journal of Educational Research, 88,* 69–85.

Morrow, L.M., & Brittain, R. (2003). The nature of storybook reading in the elementary school: Current practices. In A. van Kleeck, S.A. Stahl, & E.B. Bauer (Eds.), *On reading books to young children: Parents and teachers* (pp. 140–158). Mahwah, NJ: Erlbaum.

Parravano, M.V. (2006). It's all good. *Horn Book, 82,* 501–502.

Peterson, B. (2001). *Literary pathways: Selecting books to support new readers.* Portsmouth, NH: Heinemann.

Purves, A.C., & Rippere, V. (1968). *Elements of writing about a literary work* (Research Rep. No. 9). Urbana, IL: National Council of Teachers of English.

Rosenblatt, L.M. (1938). *Literature as exploration.* New York: D. Appleton-Century.

Rosenblatt, L.M. (1978). *The reader, the text, the poem: The transactional theory of the literary work.* Carbondale: Southern Illinois University Press.

Scarborough, H.S., & Dobrich, W. (1994). On the efficacy of reading to preschoolers. *Developmental Review, 14,* 245–302.

Sipe, L.R. (2000). The construction of literary understanding by first and second graders in oral response to picture storybook read-alouds. *Reading Research Quarterly, 35,* 252–275.

Teale, W.H. (2003). Reading aloud to young children as a classroom instructional activity: Insights from research and practice. In A. van Kleeck, S.A. Stahl, & E.B. Bauer (Eds.), *On reading books to young children: Parents and teachers* (pp. 114–139). Mahwah, NJ: Erlbaum.

Veatch, J., & Goodrich, W. (1968). *How to teach reading with children's books.* New York: Citation Press.

Wells, G. (1986). *The meaning makers: Children learning language and using language to learn.* Portsmouth, NH: Heinemann.

Wolf, S., & Heath, S.B. (1992). *The braid of literature: Children's worlds of reading.* Cambridge, MA: Harvard University Press.

CHILDREN'S LITERATURE CITED

Fitzhugh, L., & Scoppettone, S. (1969). *Bang bang you're dead.* New York: Harper.

Hamilton, V. (1974). *M.C. Higgins the great.* New York: Macmillan.

Hesse, K. (1997). *Out of the dust.* New York: Scholastic.

L'Engle, M. (1962). *A wrinkle in time.* New York: Ariel.

Lester, J. (1968). *To be a slave.* New York: Dial Books for Young Readers.

Macaulay, D. (1990). *Black and white.* Boston: Houghton Mifflin.

Martin, B., Jr. (1983). *Brown bear, brown bear, what do you see?* Austin, TX: Holt, Rinehart and Winston.

Rowling, J.K. (1998). *Harry Potter and the sorcerer's stone.* New York: Scholastic.

Scieszka, J., & Smith, L. (1989). *The true story of the three little pigs.* New York: Viking Press.

CHAPTER 9

Fifty Years of Remedial and Clinical Reading in the United States: A Historical Overview

Sandra McCormick and Judy Braithwaite

Sandra McCormick

Judy Braithwaite

Fairly early in our careers, we both worked as reading resource teachers in a large urban school district. Our job roles involved providing inservice programs, as well as intensive professional assistance, to educators in select inner-city schools—tasks very much consistent with those of today's literacy coach. During this time, we noted that classroom teachers, administrators, and parents who were searching for solutions to assist delayed readers often relied on information found in newspaper articles, advertised on television, or passed along by well-meaning but uninformed friends. In far too many cases, such programs or procedures were based on principles that research clearly had shown to be ineffective, often old ideas that long since had proven to be unsuccessful in promoting reading growth for students with low aptitudes for reading. It became apparent to us that lack of knowledge about past practices and about the history of research in this area resulted in educators and parents wasting instructional time on useless ideas when effective ideas were available to them.

An Essential History of Current Reading Practices, edited by Mary Jo Fresch.
© 2008 by the International Reading Association.

assessment, which reports strategies and tools used at that time to instruct delayed readers or to test their reading competence; and (3) milestones, which relates events that influenced the treatment of delayed readers and the profession of reading educators.

A Little Bit of Background: The 1800s Through the 1940s

To set the stage for our 50-year review, let's step back in time a bit and briefly look at certain theories and practices that were prevalent at early stages of remedial and clinical reading and, as well, note certain important milestones of those times (see Table 9.1).

Causation

In the earliest days of this discipline, much attention was given to determining the underlying cause of reading delays, with many of the first proposals seeming exceptionally quaint today. For example, in the late 1800s, difficulty in learning to read was attributed to "word blindness," which was believed to be a congenital defect. Reading-delayed individuals—whose vision was otherwise wholly intact—were thought to be unable to see print.

Table 9.1. Remedial Reading Prior to 1950

Causation	Instruction and Assessment	Milestones
1800 • Congenital word blindness		
	1910–1919 • First instructional strategy devised for nonreaders • Gray Oral Reading Test	*1910–1919* • First journal article on reading disabilities
1920 • Lack of cerebral dominance • Faulty eye movements		*1920–1929* • First reading clinic • First remedial textbook
1930 • Emotional disturbance		
1940 • Eye defects • Multiple causation	*1940–1949* • Informal Reading Inventories (IRIs)	*1940–1949* • Roots of early learning disabilities (LD) movement

During the first part of the 1950s, emotional disturbance continued to be postulated as a cause of reading delays. This explanation was so popular that psychotherapy was at times suggested as a remedial strategy. In the second half of the decade, there was a move away from emphasis on emotional causes and toward attribution of reading problems to physiological and neurological factors. Use of medications to remediate reading problems was investigated, yet none of the studies reported improvement of reading. Vernon's *Backwardness in Reading* (1957), which purported visual perception problems as the source of reading disability, influenced several instructional programs designed to remediate visual perception difficulties in the next decade, but these proved to have little utility. Delacato (1959) proposed lack of neurological organization as the origin of reading difficulties and introduced a treatment program that relied primarily on body management activities; subsequent research demonstrated that this approach was not viable.

In contrast, Flesch (1955) focused on a wholly educational cause of low reading achievement. The premise of his book *Why Johnny Can't Read* was that lack of reading progress in U.S. schools was due to the prevalence of the whole-word method of reading instruction. This influential book led to strongly re-newed attention to phonics instruction in regular classrooms and in remedial programs (see also chapters 1, 2, 5, and 7, this volume, for more discussion of Flesch's influence).

Instruction and Assessment

During this time period, a book published in the previous decade by Lamoreaux and Lee (1943) was instrumental in reviving interest in the Language Experience Approach (LEA). Originally introduced in the 1930s, LEA again found its way into many first-grade classes in the 1950s. Because this approach used the student's own language for reading text, it was deemed by many edu-cators to be an easier, more natural way to learn than through the more struc-tured basal readers of the day; thus this instructional approach was incorporated into many remedial classes.

A concern for adults who were poor readers was another distinguishing trend of this period. During both World Wars, the armed forces had found it necessary to provide special literacy training to a fairly large number of mili-tary inductees who had low reading levels. The plight of these young men heightened national awareness about the minimal educational attainment of some members of U.S. society—an awareness that, by the 1950s, led to a num-ber of adult literacy efforts. In Coach Classes, functionally illiterate individuals

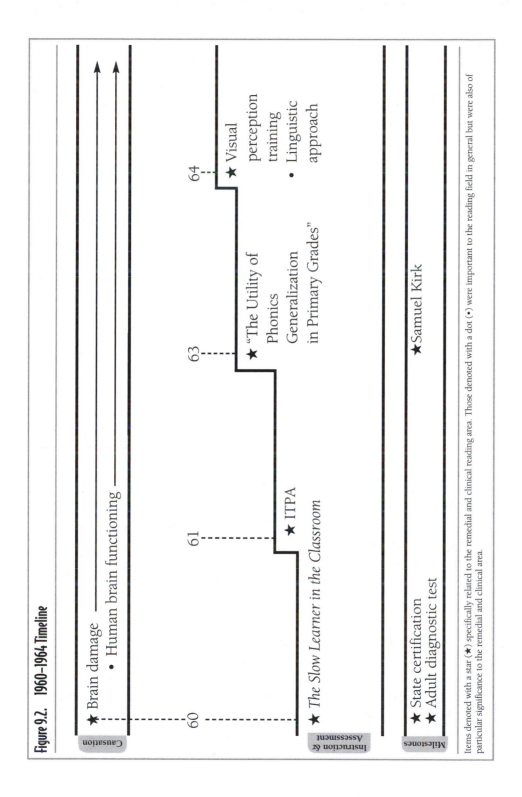

Figure 9.2. 1960–1964 Timeline

Causation

★ Brain damage
• Human brain functioning

Instruction & Assessment

The Slow Learner in the Classroom

★ ITPA

★ "The Utility of Phonics Generalization in Primary Grades"

★ Visual perception training
• Linguistic approach

60   61   63   64

Milestones

★ State certification
★ Adult diagnostic test

★ Samuel Kirk

Items denoted with a star (★) specifically related to the remedial and clinical reading area. Those denoted with a dot (•) were important to the reading field in general but were also of particular significance to the remedial and clinical area.

Table 9.2. Terms Used to Describe Students With Learning Disabilities	
Prior to 1963	**After 1963**
• Brain injured	• Learning disabled
• Childhood aphasics	
• Children with cerebral dysfunction	
• Children with perceptual-motor handicaps	
• Children with strephosymbolia	
• Congenitally word blind	
• Developmentally dyslexic	
• Dyslexic	
• Minimally brain damaged	
• Children with minimal brain dysfunction	
• Neurological disorder	
• Neurological impairment	
• Perceptually disabled	
• Perceptually handicapped	
• Psychoneurological disability	
• Strauss-syndrome children	

McCormick, S. (2003). *Instructing students who have literacy problems* (4th ed., p. 11). Upper Saddle River, NJ: Pearson Education Inc. Reprinted with permission.

Milestones

A milestone of note in the early 1960s resulted from special educator Samuel Kirk's suggestion that the many labels currently in use for persons with the same types of learning difficulties be collapsed into one, leading to adoption of the term *learning disabilities* or *learning disabled* in the special education field. Table 9.2 shows the array of terms once used by the education community. This also was the time when state certification for reading teachers began, and the first reading diagnostic tests especially for adults were designed.

1965 Through 1969: From Title I to *Reading Research Quarterly*

As with the first half of the 1960s, many theories, as well as practices, of the second half of the decade focused on physiological variables. (See the timeline in Figure 9.3.)

Causation

Hypotheses on causes of reading difficulties proposed in the early part of the 1960s—brain damage and divergent brain functioning—continued to be accepted as somewhat likely possibilities during the second half of the decade, with the addition of yet another possible physiological contributor: visual–motor defects. This hypothesis stated that lack of eye–hand coordination and other factors of coordination were thought to underlie reading problems.

Instruction and Assessment

Three instructional methods of this era have not stood up to research. Getman (1965) advocated training oculo–motor control to remediate assumed visual–motor deficits; students in some LD classes, remedial reading classes, and clinics were required to engage in activities in which, in a variety of ways, they followed moving targets with their eyes. Also of questionable value was a program based on Delacato's (1959) theory from the decade before, which contended that lack of neurological organization was the root of reading disability. This program included, among other activities, crawling and creeping on the floor—notably peculiar forms of reading remediation. Private clinics opened that employed these procedures, and parents paid to enroll their children. Several research investigations made important contributions during the second half of the 1960s when researchers clearly refuted claims that this program had academic value.

A third notion of the time that has not passed the research test was the supposition that students could learn to read more readily if they were taught through their strongest modality. After assessment that purportedly could identify just what an individual's preferred modality was, procedures were compiled that were alleged to be more visually oriented for students with a strong "visual aptitude," more auditorily oriented for those with a strong "auditory aptitude," more tactile for those with a strong "tactile aptitude," and so on. Investigations with reading disabled students, learning disabled students, and mildly retarded students have repeatedly failed to confirm this premise.

Approaches summarized in the previous paragraphs of this section represent views of the past (occasional exceptions are the few professionals—perhaps unfamiliar with the negative research findings—who have held out hope for the "preferred modality" thesis). Despite the foregoing proposals for unusual approaches to remediation, most reading teachers of the 1960s continued to use the typical, more effective paths for reading instruction in which reading of connected text and practice with word learning and comprehension were the focal points of the program.

The 1970s: From Multiple Causation to *Sesame Street*

The 1970s brought us that great chronicle *Star Wars*. While Han Solo and Luke Skywalker clashed with Darth Vader, we continued to look for better understanding of reading difficulties and delays. (See the timeline in Figure 9.4.)

Causation

During this decade, while defective memory processes were proposed as a cause of reading problems, multiple causation still remained the belief of most reading professionals. There was much theorizing and research related to (a) studying brain behaviors occurring during reading, (b) understanding beginning reading, and (c) investigating how written text itself aids or deters reading. While these studies were targeted for the literacy field in general, educators concerned with delayed readers found much in this research that informed our understanding of reading growth and reading difficulty.

During the 1970s, two important articles related to the origins of reading delays appeared in *Reading Research Quarterly*. One was a review of research on perinatal causes—that is, possible factors occurring prior to or at birth—that might affect aptitude for reading. Published in 1975 (Balow, Rubin, & Rosen, 1975/1976), this review concluded that most studies dealing with perinatal issues in relation to reading were methodologically faulty, but two variables merited further investigation—specifically, effects on reading delay due to low birth weight and premature birth. These two issues have more recently gathered attention in the LD field. Near the end of the decade, Valtin's (1978/1979) "Dyslexia: Deficit in Reading or Deficit in Research?" pointed out inadequacies in many investigations on reading disabilities that made results questionable. Furthermore, Valtin's article has positively influenced the quality of research in this area since.

Instruction and Assessment

Use of the LEA with poor readers continued, but a second strong interest involved diagnostic/prescriptive teaching. This latter instructional method was quite different from LEA, because specific reading objectives were stated, students were pretested to determine which ones they had not mastered, and teaching strategies were keyed to those specific objectives. A third emphasis was instruction based on Goodman's Reading Model (Goodman, 1967, 1970; see also chapters 1, 2, 5, 6, 8, and 10, this volume, for more discussion of Goodman's contributions) and psycholinguistic theory, leading to changes in many remedial classes, with focus centered more on reading for meaning and less on word-perfect oral reading (see also chapters 1, 2, and 5, this volume, for more discussion of psycholinguistics).

In 1971, the first of many studies that refuted process training appeared (Bateman, 1971; Hammill & Larsen, 1974; Masland & Cratty, 1971; Saphier, 1973). These investigations indicated that body management activities and the training of visual processing and auditory processing had no effect on reading achievement. Eventually, these studies brought about major changes in LD programming.

The following year, Goodman and Burke (1972) published *Reading Miscue Inventory* (RMI) based on the then-popular Goodman Reading Model. This inventory, an important diagnostic tool in remedial classes for a time, emphasized the role of meaning when assessing reading errors (also referred to as *miscues*). Teachers using this test no longer merely *counted* miscues—as commonly done with older instruments—but instead considered the degree to which each oral reading error did or did not disrupt understanding of the text.

Concurrently, understanding of text meanings also became the focus of much reading research. Traditional comprehension instruction began to be challenged by these studies, ultimately bringing about changes in how teachers provided comprehension instruction to both average and poor readers (see also Chapter 5, this volume, for further discussion of comprehension instruction).

Milestones

During this decade, federal initiatives fostered several literacy efforts. In 1970, a forerunner of the No Child Left Behind Act of 2001 was begun. This effort, the federally funded National Right-to-Read Program, heightened interest in reading instruction but failed to meet its goals for eradication of reading problems in the United States. In 1975, Public Law 94-142, the Education for All Handicapped Children Act, was passed, strengthening educational requirements for learning disabled and other special education students.

In a continuing effort to find ways that television—the principal visual medium of the day—could be harnessed for educational uses, federal backing and creative development resulted in two popular television programs, *Sesame Street* and *The Electric Company*, both designed to promote reading growth.

Figure 9.5. 1980–1989 Timeline

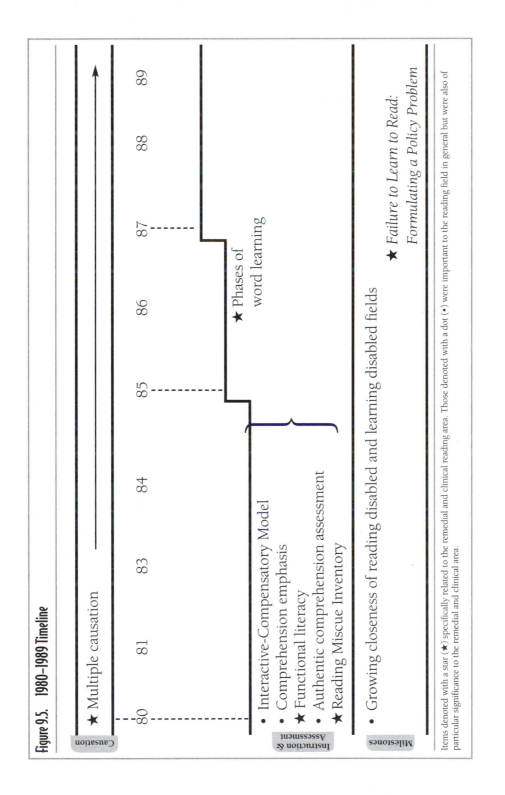

Causation

★ Multiple causation

80 81 83 84 85 86 87 88 89

★ Phases of
word learning

**Instruction &
Assessment**

- Interactive-Compensatory Model
- Comprehension emphasis
- ★ Functional literacy
- Authentic comprehension assessment
- ★ Reading Miscue Inventory

Milestones

- Growing closeness of reading disabled and learning disabled fields

★ *Failure to Learn to Read:
Formulating a Policy Problem*

Items denoted with a star (★) specifically related to the remedial and clinical reading area. Those denoted with a dot (•) were important to the reading field in general but were also of particular significance to the remedial and clinical area.

Figure 9.6. 1990-1999 Timeline

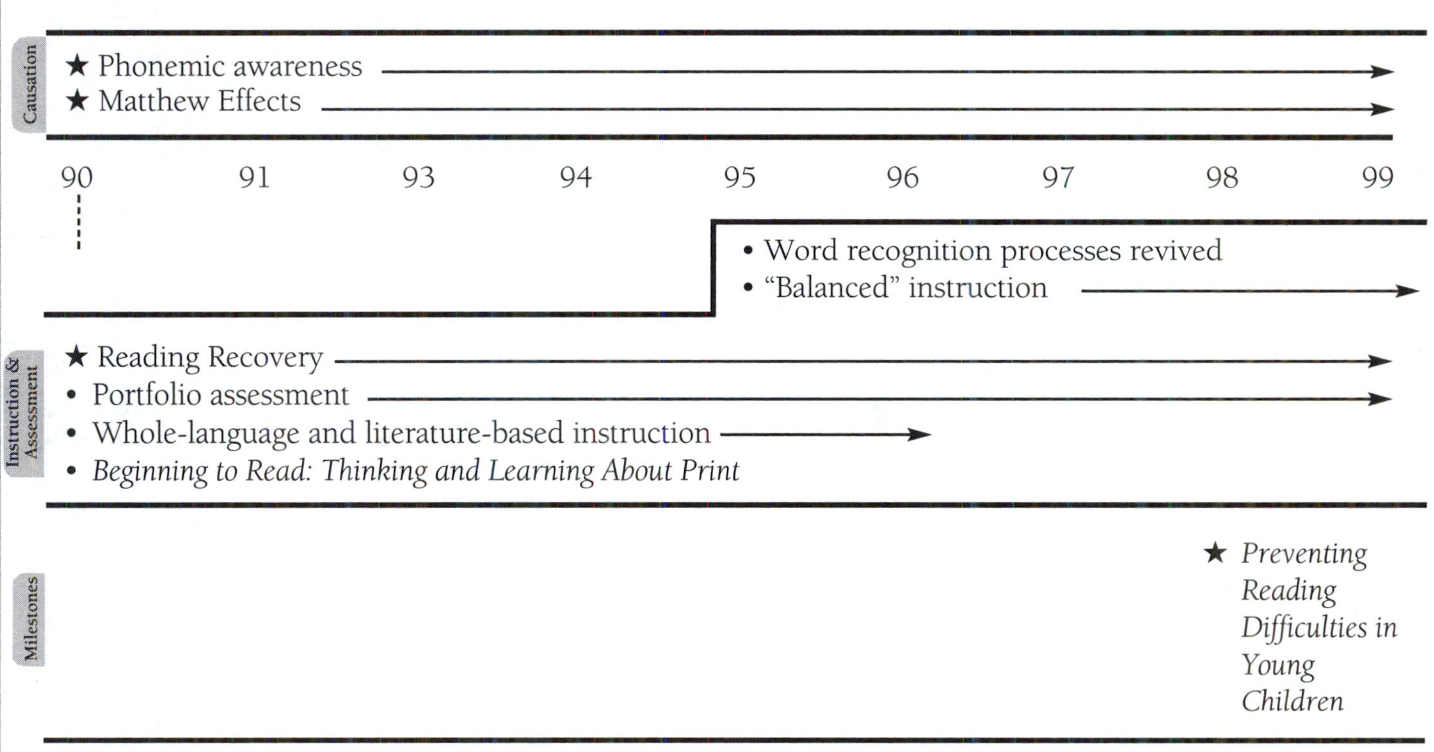

	90	91	92	93	94	95	96	97	98	99

Causation

★ Phonemic awareness ——————————→
★ Matthew Effects ——————————→

Instruction & Assessment

• Word recognition processes revived
• "Balanced" instruction ——————————————→

★ Reading Recovery ——————————————————————→
• Portfolio assessment ——————————————————————→
• Whole-language and literature-based instruction ——————→
• *Beginning to Read: Thinking and Learning About Print*

Milestones

★ *Preventing Reading Difficulties in Young Children*

Items denoted with a star (★) specifically related to the remedial and clinical reading area. Those denoted with a dot (•) were important to the reading field in general but were also of particular significance to the remedial and clinical area.

struggling readers because the process that is involved permits ongoing evaluation of changing student needs, as well as a comprehensive documentation of student progress—both important considerations for delayed readers.

Milestones

An important highlight of this decade was the publication of a major report, *Preventing Reading Difficulties in Young Children* (Snow, Burns, & Griffin, 1998). This book provided an informed and reasoned discussion of research and contained large numbers of research-derived recommendations for reading instruction that spoke directly to what teachers need to know to work effectively with average readers and with delayed readers. The many recommendations addressed sound reading instruction for the primary grades, research-based literacy development for the preschool and kindergarten years, the teaching of reading to language-minority children, instruction for students with persistent reading delays, the education of teachers of reading, and resources for instruction. This book continues to be influential today.

2000 Through 2007: From the National Reading Panel Report to No Child Left Behind

This new century has brought us the tragedy of 9/11, exercises to keep our brains young, and the best day on Wall Street since the 1980s. Our attitudes have changed about who we are and what we can do: We do not retire but reinvent ourselves; we text message, rather than call or write; and we move in a smaller world—through the Web—like a flash of lightning.

At the time this chapter was prepared, a full decade into the new millennium had not elapsed, so it is too early to identify all distinguishing events and trends in the area of remedial and clinical reading. We can, however, look at what has captured our attention and energies in the first years.

Causation

In regard to causal issues, research continues to offer strong evidence of the role of phonemic awareness in reading delay. In addition, early in the decade, the growing availability of technologies such as PET scans and MRIs for examining brain behaviors revived some interest in the relationship of neurobiological factors to reading difficulties. To date, criticisms of this work have pointed out an inconsistency in the quality of the research associated with these explorations.

other teachers in professional development. This role has, in large part, been responsible for helping good classroom teachers increase their expertise for working with delayed readers in their classes.

Necessarily, because of NCLB, much assessment of struggling readers at the present time is in large part tied to state standards. This has led to continuing tensions over "low-stakes" testing—in which assessment of delayed readers primarily provides information on students' specific instructional needs—versus "high-stakes" testing—in which assessment's primary purpose is to document whether school districts are raising student reading achievement, that is, whether low-achieving pupils are making adequate yearly progress, as defined by NCLB.

Not a new issue, but one that has been further—and strongly—highlighted by the NCLB initiative, is the English-language learners who are delayed readers because of their bilingual and bicultural literacy challenges. Because the 1990s saw the largest number of immigrants of all time entering the United States, this issue has become a major one in the 2000s, even in communities where, until recently, *new* immigrants had not traditionally settled.

Future Directions

We would like to offer a brief wish list for the remainder of this decade. In an article in *Reading Research Quarterly*, Baumann and colleagues (Baumann, Hoffman, Duffy-Hester, & Ro, 2000) compared teacher responses to questions about reading instruction posed in *The First R* (Austin & Morrison, 1963) with teachers' responses to the same questions today. In both time periods, regular classroom teachers said that understanding how to help the struggling readers in their classes was their biggest problem. Our first wish is that all teachers take coursework for dealing with these students, including clinical practice in which they roll up their sleeves and concentrate one-to-one, with close supervisory help, on learning effective remedial and clinical reading strategies.

In addition, we are gravely concerned about the lack of research on effective instructional strategies for our most severe cases of reading delay. Although a large amount of data are available to guide instruction of mildly and moderately delayed readers, severely delayed readers have been given little attention. When one examines the general population or the student population, it is evident that the number of severely delayed readers is proportionally much smaller than those with mild and moderate reading delays. However, one must remember that severely delayed readers are the students with the most crucial needs. Although they are usually of average intelligence or above, without special assistance these students are quite likely to be functionally illiterate or

McCormick, S. (2007). *Instructing students who have literacy problems* (5th ed.). Upper Saddle River, NJ: Merrill/Prentice Hall.

Michael, P.A., & Dougherty, C. (1999). Reading clinic: Past, present, and...future? In P.B. Mosenthal & D.H. Evensen (Eds.), *Advance in reading/language research* (Vol. 6, pp. 365–384). London: JAI Press.

Pelosi, P.L. (1977). The roots of reading diagnosis. In H.A. Robinson (Ed.), *Reading and writing in America: Historical trends* (pp. 69–75). Newark, DE: International Reading Association.

Pelosi, P.L. (1981). The disabled reader in years past. *Journal of Research and Development in Education, 14,* 1–10.

Smith, N.B. (2002). *American reading instruction* (Special ed.). Newark, DE: International Reading Association.

Spear-Swerling, L., & Sternberg, R.J. (1998). The history of LD: Variations on a theme. In L. Spear-Swerling & R.J. Sternberg (Eds.), *Off-track: When poor readers become "learning disabled"* (pp. 29–52). Boulder, CO: Westview Press.

REFERENCES

Adams, M.J. (1990). *Beginning to read: Thinking and learning about print.* Cambridge, MA: MIT Press.

Austin, M.C., & Morrison, C. (1963). *The first R: The Harvard report on reading in elementary schools.* New York: Macmillan.

Ball, E.W. & Blachman, B.A. (1991). Does phoneme awareness training in kindergarten make a difference in early word recognition and developmental spelling? *Reading Research Quarterly, 26,* 49–66.

Balow, B., Rubin, R., & Rosen, M.J. (1975–1976). Perinatal events as precursors of reading disabilities. *Reading Research Quarterly, 11,* 36–71.

Bateman, B. (1971). The role of individual diagnosis in remedial planning for reading disorders. In E.O. Calkins (Ed.), *Reading forum* (NINDS Monograph No. 11). Bethesda, MD: National Institute of Neurological Diseases and Strokes.

Baumann, J.F., Hoffman, J.V., Duffy-Hester, A.M., &Ro, J.M. (2000). "The first R" yesterday and today: U.S. elementary reading instruction practices reported by teachers and administrators. *Reading Research Quarterly, 35,* 338–377.

Clay, M.M. (1972). *The early detection of reading difficulties: A diagnostic survey.* Auckland, New Zealand: Heinemann.

Clymer, T. (1963). The utility of phonics generalizations in the primary grades. *The Reading Teacher, 16,* 252–258.

Cook, W.D. (1977). *Adult literacy education in the United States.* Newark, DE: International Reading Association.

De Hirsch, K., Jansky, J.J., & Langford, W.S. (1966). *Predicting reading failure: A preliminary study of reading, writing, and spelling.* New York: Harper & Row.

Delacato, C.H. (1959). *The treatment and prevention of reading problems: The neuro-psychological approach.* Springfield, IL: Thomas.

Ehri, L. (1987). Learning to read and spell words. *Journal of Reading Behavior, 19,* 5–31.

Ehri, L., & Wilce, L.S. (1985). Movement into reading: Is the first stage of printed word learning visual or phonetic? *Reading Research Quarterly, 20,* 163–179.

Ehri, L., & Wilce, L. (1987). Cipher versus cue reading: An experiment in decoding acquisition. *Journal of Educational Psychology, 79,* 3–13.

Stanovich, K.E. (1986). Matthew effects in reading: Some consequences of individual differences in the acquisition of literacy. *Reading Research Quarterly, 21,* 360–407.

Sulzby, E., & Teale, W. (1991). Emergent literacy. In R. Barr, M.L. Kamil. P. Mosenthal, & P.D. Pearson (Eds.), *Handbook of reading research* (Vol. 2, pp. 727–758). New York: Longman.

Uhl, W.L. (1916). The use of the results of reading tests as bases for planning remedial work. *The Elementary School Journal, 17,* 266–275.

Vellutino, F.R., & Denckla, M.B. (1991). Cognitive and neuropsychological foundations of word identification in poor and normally developing readers. In R. Barr, M.L. Kamil, P. Mosentahl, & P.D. Pearson (Eds.), *Handbook of reading research* (Vol. 2, pp. 571–608). New York: Longman.

Vernon, M.D. (1957). *Backwardness in reading: A study of its nature and origin.* Cambridge, England: Cambridge University Press.

Valtin, R. (1978/1979). Dyslexia: Deficit in reading or deficit in research. *Reading Research Quarterly, 14,* 201–221.

My interest in vocabulary grew out of the connections between spelling and meaning for "higher-level" words derived from Latin and Greek roots, but it quickly expanded as I read reports and reviews that stressed the importance of vocabulary size across all grade levels and as I collected informal evidence from tutors and students in my role as director of the Ohio State University Reading Clinic.

This chapter is divided into three sections. The first reviews various aspects of spelling and how our understandings about them have changed over time. The second section focuses on changing ideas about vocabulary. The final section suggests future directions in research and instruction for both spelling and vocabulary.

Changing Perspectives on Spelling

As with other aspects of language and literacy learning, through the late 1960s scholarship on learning to spell and spelling instruction was heavily influenced by traditional views and behavioristic perspectives. Accordingly, English spelling was analyzed as being highly irregular because of the inconsistent nature of grapheme–phoneme and phoneme–grapheme correspondences. Therefore rote memorization was considered the best means of learning and teaching. Frequency and usage were primary in determining the content and order of instruction. Further, spelling and word recognition were seen as separate processes and generally taught separately.

For the most part, research and development efforts were consistent with these understandings. In their comprehensive review of the literature on spelling difficulty, Cahen, Craun, and Johnson (1970) concluded that much of the research and development up to that time focused on (a) determining the number of occurrences of words in student writings in order to develop frequency-based lists for efficient study, (b) creating lists of "demon words" that were found to give students the most difficulty in writing, and (c) determining which study routines (e.g., study-test vs. test-study-test; peer-correction vs. self-correction) are most successful and efficient. While these works did provide useful information about surface characteristics, they contributed little to our understanding of the process of learning to spell. For example, those constructing demon lists were often at a loss to explain why a sound–letter correspondence might be spelled correctly in one word but pose serious difficulty in another. Gates's (1937) collection and organization of elementary-grade

that preserves meaning units over time and place as pronunciations vary (for example, -ed remains the regular spelling of past tense even though in certain phonological environments the pronunciation has been reduced to /d/ or /t/). He also asserted that because sound changes tend to be systematic, the relationships between sound and spelling are also systematic but often quite complex and not intuitively obvious.

Two conclusions to be drawn from these analyses are the following:

1. English orthography becomes more sensible and predictable when visual, meaning, and historical patterns as well as letter–sound relationships are taken into consideration (often now discussed as layers of alphabet, pattern, meaning, and origin).

2. Making sense of these complex but systematic relationships requires time, experience, and a growing understanding of how words work.

New Understandings of Spelling

It was in the context of these new ideas that educational researchers and scholars, including Ed Henderson, his associates, and his students, were striving to make sense of young children's spellings. But they lacked a key piece to the puzzle: the thorough knowledge of English phonology necessary to understand the logic in young children's attempts.

In the 1970s, Read (1971, 1975) brought this knowledge to his analysis of preschool children's spellings. He argued that the children in his studies seemed to use a letter–name strategy, that is, they often represented the phonemes they heard in words by matching them to the names of the letters they knew. But because of particular aspects of those relationships in English, they generated spellings that did not match the expectations of adults, who are typically "biased" by their knowledge of the conventional system. Some of the patterns that Read observed included

a. The use of h to represent the ch spelling, as in child

b. The use of j or g for d and h or ch for t, but mostly in r blends, as in dragon and track

c. Nasal omissions, but only when nasals function as part of a consonant blend, as in send and bump

d. The use of the "closest" long vowel (i.e., vowel name) to represent short vowels, because short-vowel sounds do not function as letter names in English—for example, e for i in fit, a for e in egg, i for o in hot

replicating many of Read's findings but also seeing other patterns as well (Beers & Henderson, 1977; Gentry, 1982; Treiman, 1993). In the spirit of the times, the focus was often on celebrating the inventiveness of student spellings.

Over time, a more longitudinal perspective emerged, with a focus on how children move from invention to convention as they are influenced by their language environment, literacy experiences, and school instruction. Through an ongoing, sustained set of studies grounded in the collection and analysis of student correct and incorrect spellings and reading behaviors, Henderson, his colleagues, and students (sometimes referred to as the Virginia School; Treiman, 1993) developed and refined the concept of developmental stages of word knowledge, also known as stage theory (e.g., Henderson, 1981; Henderson & Beers, 1980; Morris, 1989a, 1989b; Templeton & Bear, 1992).

The following stages and brief descriptions (from Scharer & Zutell, 2003) are now well known in both the research and instructional literature:

1. Prephonetic/Prealphabetic, characterized by letter strings that represent concepts and ideas but without a discernable match between letters and sounds

2. Semiphonetic/Early Alphabetic, characterized in the early part by the use of single consonants to represent beginning or particularly salient sounds in the word; over time children include letters for both beginning and ending sounds, with long vowels generally represented before short ones

3. Letter Name/Phonetic/Alphabetic, characterized by the ability to consistently match first-to-last in spoken words with left-to-right in the written forms, generally representing each phoneme in a word, regularly with the logic Read described

4. Within Word Pattern/Transitional, characterized by correct spelling of well-known words and single consonants and many blend and consonant digraph patterns, and by good control of short-vowel patterns; at this stage children begin to include visual features like vowel markers and other silent letter patterns into their spellings

5. Syllable Juncture, in which students grapple with patterns for combining syllables, including consonant doubling and e-drop patterns

6. Derivational Constancy, in which students deal with the morphological patterns in English multisyllabic words whose pronunciations often obscure the links in meaning and spelling among words in the same root–word families (e.g., *cave–cavity–excavation*)

Reading–Spelling Connections

Traditionally, word recognition and spelling have been treated as separate processes. Of course, both share the same writing system, but it was thought that going from print to sound is distinctly different than going from sound to print. That is, recognition is more directly supported by context and can be completed successfully using partial cues from the letters in a word, whereas context usually does not aid the writer in producing a correct spelling, at least not to the same degree. Sound–letter correspondences are not simply the reverse of letter–sound correspondences and are not necessarily equally distributed. For example, in reading/pronunciation, *f* almost always is pronounced /f/, but in spelling, /f/ is fairly often represented by *ph* as well as *f*. Further, there seem to be many examples of good readers who are poor spellers. In fact, the prestigious *Handbook of Reading Research* did not include a chapter on spelling (Templeton & Morris, 2000) until its third volume.

However, researchers and educators have come to understand that the connections between word learning for reading and spelling are much closer than previously recognized. Although the stages described above are often discussed with reference to spelling, Henderson and his associates (e.g., see Templeton & Bear, 1992) have framed them as stages of word knowledge because they assert that there is a significant and direct relationship between word knowledge for reading and word knowledge for spelling. For example, Morris and Perney (1984) found high significant correlations between midyear spelling scores based on a developmental scale and the acquisition of a sight vocabulary by the end of the year for first-grade students. Results of subsequent studies (Morris, 1993; Morris, Bloodgood, Lomax, & Perney, 2003) have shown significant sequential interactive relationships among beginning consonant knowledge, concept of word (voice-pointing), phonemic segmentation (measured both with oral and spelling tasks), and the acquisition of a sight vocabulary for beginning readers.

Young children's spelling attempts in both formal and informal contexts require phonemic segmentation and so serve as both a means of assessment and practice of phonemic awareness, a skill now considered essential to the development of fluent reading (National Institute of Child Health and Human Development, 2000; see also Adams, 1990). One might even argue it is a more natural measure than some of the tasks in current use. In both cross-sectional and longitudinal studies, Zutell (1992; Zutell & Fresch, 1991; Zutell & Rasinski, 1989) found strong positive correlations among a developmental spelling measure, fluency, and word recognition, both in and out of context, for

in the hustle and bustle of classroom activities, teachers may be unaware of how students have produced correct spellings. Students may have written words from memory, copied from a word wall or other classroom source, or asked a classmate for help. While these may all be excellent pragmatic solutions, they limit what can be determined from such spellings.

Similarly, selecting words from writing, even when supplemented with high-frequency lists, may deal with immediate concerns but fail to address students' developmental needs in a focused, systematic way. This approach also places high demands on teacher time and knowledge for analyzing errors, seeing patterns in performance, and choosing which words to teach. School systems have not always been willing to invest the time and resources necessary to build teacher competence. Uninformed and unsupported teachers may choose inappropriate words for instruction, resort to traditional materials, or reduce the time and energy put into word study. And a lack of a consistent whole-school/district philosophy and approach can lead to inconsistent instruction both across grades and across classrooms at the same grade level, a potential source of confusion and frustration for teachers, students, and parents.

> Uninformed and unsupported teachers may choose inappropriate words for instruction, resort to traditional materials, or reduce the time and energy put into word study.

Many scholars and educators who follow a developmental perspective have offered a different approach. They recognize the importance of student writing generally and as a source of information about spelling specifically, but they also stress the value of assessing students more directly to determine their developmental stages and/or instructional levels so as to focus instruction at those levels (Morris, Blanton, Blanton, Nowacek, & Perney, 1995).

One result has been the construction of a variety of assessment instruments that are organized around stages and levels (Bear, Invernizzi, Templeton, & Johnston, 2000; Fresch & Wheaton, 2002; Ganske, 2000; Schlagal, 1989, 1992). Words are chosen for their frequency, familiarity, and/or relevance to the curriculum but also for features whose spellings reveal students' stages. For example, students at beginning levels are tested on words embodying short-vowel patterns, *dr-/tr-* blends, and nasal blends (see the description of Read's findings above). Spellers who have sufficiently mastered these features are tested on various long-vowel patterns, words with -*ed* endings, and so forth, while students at higher levels are tested on words involving joining syllables (*e*-drop, consonant doubling), then complex derivational patterns. Words are scored for how salient features are spelled as well as for correctness. Student profiles built from this information reveal a pattern of student strengths and weaknesses. These are then used to inform small-group and/or individual instruction.

base, Romance vocabulary imported with the Norman invasion and later through further interactions with French, literary and academic words built from Latin and Greek elements, adoptions and adaptations from other languages, and words made from other formation processes (such as toponyms, eponyms, portmanteau words).

Combining morphemic elements both within and across the major contributing language families is a significant process for building English words. Estimates indicate that, in written text, words with affixes outnumber single-morpheme words by a ratio of 4:1 (Wysocki & Jenkins, 1987); more than half the words in school English are formed by suffixation, prefixation, and compounding; and/or 60% of the new words acquired by school-age children are morphologically complex but with relatively transparent morphological structures, such that the meanings of the parts provide strong clues to the meaning of the whole word (Nagy & Anderson, 1989; Nagy, Anderson, & Diakidoy, 1993).

For many words learned beyond primary grades, the relationships between pronunciations and spellings can be particularly complex. Grapheme–phoneme correspondences from foreign and even Greek derived words may not always follow typical English patterns (e.g., *ch* = /k/ as in *anarchy*, the "long e" pronunciation at the end of *catastrophe*). The process of prefix assimilation (*in* + *legal* = *illegal*, not *inlegal*) can obscure the prefix for the reader and create spelling difficulties (double letter) for the writer.

Further, stress patterns in English multisyllabic words are complex and not indicated by grapheme–phoneme relationships. And the unequal assignment of stress among syllables often results in unstressed vowels, obscuring the meaning elements within words. To take a simple example, in *thermometer* primary stress falls on the second syllable with little stress on the last two, with syllable division after the second /m/. The result is that the relationship between the meaning units, *thermo* (heat) and *meter* (measure), is hidden in pronunciation. On the other hand, according to the principle of derivational constancy, words derived from the same roots tend to maintain similar spellings even though pronunciations vary because of syllable patterns and stress (e.g., *cave–cavity–excavation*). Thus, at these complex levels, spelling and meaning are closely intertwined.

Instructional Issues

The size and complexity of this system would seem to put considerable demands upon students' acquiring a literate vocabulary and a high level of reading achievement. Lexical access, that is access to the meanings of words, is a key to successful reading (Beck, Perfetti, & McKeown, 1982). In primary grades, the

sometimes misleading unless you know a lot about the word beforehand (Schatz & Baldwin, 1986). Nagy, Herman, and Anderson (1985) suggested that of 100 unfamiliar words met in reading, only 5–15 of them will be learned at that encounter. An effective approach to vocabulary learning will include the regular and direct teaching of a chosen set of words. These words will not only be important in themselves, but they will also serve as anchors and examples for independent learning. Regular instruction keeps students focused on the importance of word learning and gives them the tools to unlock word meanings as they encounter new words in their assigned and independent reading (Zutell, 2004/2005).

Traditional vocabulary instruction is based on a skill-and-drill model, often with little clarity as to the word selection process and with multiple-choice, fill-in-the-blank, and look-it-up-in-the-dictionary assignments as the major instructional activities. Findings from instructional research have suggested that such an approach is insufficient to effectively promote student learning (e.g., Stahl, 1999). In their review of the literature, Blachowicz and Fisher (2000) suggested four research-supported principles that should be incorporated to make a vocabulary program effective: (1) students should be actively involved in word learning, (2) word learning should include a personalized component, (3) students should be immersed in words, and (4) multiple sources and repeated exposures should be incorporated in instruction. Effective instruction also includes teaching word learning strategies such as using context clues, using word parts, and using the dictionary and other reference sources. As with spelling instruction, there are now a number of professional texts that provide teachers with both the research foundations and practical resources and materials to put a research-based approach into action in their classrooms (e.g., Blachowicz & Fisher, 2006; Graves, 2006; Stahl & Nagy, 2006; see also Dale, O'Rourke, & Bamman, 1971).

Early Vocabulary Development

Since their beginnings, most vocabulary research and instruction have focused on students in middle and high school grades, with some interest in upper elementary grades, propelled by the concept of the "fourth-grade slump" noted above, because those were the grade levels at which a direct connection between vocabulary and reading achievement could be seen. Recently, however, we have learned much more about the impact of early vocabulary development for later achievement and the significant differences in vocabulary sizes between young at-risk children and their peers. For example, Cunningham and Stanovich (1997) found a strong relationship between oral vocabulary in first grade and reading achievement at eleventh. In their study of young children at three socioeconomic

Spelling difficulties of poor spellers and techniques for working with them deserve further study. Given recent work on brain activity and phonemic awareness, it is likely that similar studies will inform our understanding of mental activities and processes engaged during spelling. It would be useful to compare and contrast the spelling patterns of poor spellers who are poor readers with those of poor spellers who are good readers to gain a greater understanding of the learning process.

We also need fuller descriptions of the spelling patterns of learners dealing with more than one language—bilingual, English as a second language, and English as a foreign language learners—and, within these groups, those also learning other orthographies. Most spelling studies have focused on students learning English orthography. But a growing number of them are available from languages with different orthographic systems, including alphabetic, syllabic, and logographic systems and hybrids. Comparisons across such systems and populations can provide information about features and processes that may be more or less universal and ones that are more likely writing/speaking system specific.

Internet technology has created new contexts for writing with their own constraints, supports, and possibilities. These often operate outside traditional literacy environments like school and the formal white-collar workplace. Automatic spell-checkers often assist in generating correct spellings, but sometimes they create as many problems as they solve. Users have, on their own, modified traditional orthography with widely known shorthand expressions and icons. And users have varying senses as to the formality of these different writing situations. E-mail, text messages, and blogs are new sources for observing the impact of changing conditions on the orthography and its users— fertile ground for future spelling research.

Vocabulary

Many of the issues affecting the direction of spelling research and instruction are relevant and of continuing importance to vocabulary as well—in particular, those relating to at-risk learners, nonnative speakers, cross-language connections, and practicable translations from theory to practice. However, whereas for spelling changing perspectives began with young learners and then were applied to older students, for vocabulary earlier work focused on older learners; only recently has significant attention been given to the vocabulary learning of very young children. No doubt there will be continuing interest in this area with particular attention to the following:

the support of focused, organized instruction. Such instruction need not be skill and drill. It can and should be student-centered, informative, useful, and engaging. Over the years, reading educators have developed materials and activities informed by and consistent with these new understandings. Directions for the future should thus include preparing informed and enthusiastic teachers who effectively deliver the word study instruction their students need and deserve.

ESSENTIAL READINGS ON SPELLING AND VOCABULARY

Baumann, J., Kame'enui, E., & Ash, G. (2003). Research on vocabulary instruction: Voltaire redux. In J. Flood, D. Lapp, J. Squire, & J. Jenson (Eds.), *Handbook of research on teaching the English language arts* (pp. 752–785). Mahwah, NJ: Erlbaum.

Blachowicz, C., & Fisher, P. (2000). Vocabulary instruction. In M. Kamil, P. Mosenthal, P.D. Pearson, & R. Barr (Eds.), *Handbook of reading research* (Vol. 3, pp. 503–523). Mahwah, NJ: Erlbaum.

Hart, B., & Risley, T. (1995). *Meaningful differences in the everyday experience of young American children*. Baltimore: Brookes.

Henderson, E.H. (1981). *Learning to read and spell: The child's knowledge of words*. DeKalb: Northern Illinois University Press.

Henderson, E.H., & Beers, J.W. (Eds.). (1980). *Developmental and cognitive aspects of learning to spell: A reflection of word knowledge*. Newark, DE: International Reading Association.

Invernizzi, M., Abouseid, M., & Gill, T. (1994). Using students' invented spellings as a guide for spelling instruction that emphasizes word study. *The Elementary School Journal, 95*, 155–167.

Morris, D., Bloodgood, J.W., Lomax, R.G., & Perney, J. (2003). Developmental steps in learning to read: A longitudinal study in kindergarten and first grade. *Reading Research Quarterly, 38*, 302–328.

Read, C. (1971). Pre-school children's knowledge of English phonology. *Harvard Educational Review, 41*(1), 1–34.

Templeton, S., & Bear, D. (Eds.). (1992). *Development of orthographic knowledge and the foundations of literacy: A memorial festschrift of Edmund H. Henderson*. Hillsdale, NJ: Erlbaum.

Templeton, S., & Morris, D. (2000). Spelling. In M.L. Kamil, P.B. Mosenthal, P.D. Pearson, & R. Barr (Eds.), *Handbook of reading research* (Vol. 3, pp. 525–543). Mahwah, NJ: Erlbaum.

Fresch, M.J., & Wheaton, A. (1997). Sort, search, and discover: Spelling in the child-centered classroom. *The Reading Teacher, 51*, 20–31.

Fresch, M.J., & Wheaton, A. (2002). *Teaching and assessing spelling*. New York: Scholastic.

Ganske, K. (2000). *Word journeys: Assessment-guided phonics, spelling and vocabulary instruction*. New York: Guilford.

Gates, A. (1937). *A list of spelling difficulties in 3876 words*. New York: Teachers College Press.

Gentry, J. (1982). An analysis of developmental spelling in GNYS AT WRK. *The Reading Teacher, 36*, 192–200.

Goodman, K. (1969). Analysis of oral reading miscues: Applied psycholinguistics. *Reading Research Quarterly, 5*, 9–30.

Goswami, U. (2001). Early phonological development and the acquisition of literacy. In S.B. Neuman & D.K. Dickinson (Eds.), *Handbook of early literacy research* (pp. 111–125). New York: Guilford.

Graves, D. (1978). We won't let them write: Research update. *Language Arts, 55*, 635–640.

Graves, M. (2006). *The vocabulary book: Learning and instruction*. New York: Teachers College Press.

Hanna, P., Hanna, J., Hodges, R., & Rudorph, E. (1966). *Phoneme grapheme correspondences as cues to spelling improvement*. Washington, DC: U.S. Government Printing Office.

Hart, B., & Risley, T. (1995). *Meaningful differences in the everyday experience of young American children*. Baltimore: Brookes.

Henderson, E.H. (1981). *Learning to read and spell: The child's knowledge of words*. DeKalb, IL: Northern Illinois University Press.

Henderson, E.H. (1992). The interface of lexical competence and knowledge of written words. In S. Templeton & D.R. Bear (Eds.), *Development of orthographic knowledge and the foundations of literacy: A memorial festschrift for Edmund H. Henderson* (pp. 1–30). Hillsdale, NJ: Erlbaum.

Henderson, E.H., & Beers, J.W. (Eds.). (1980). *Developmental and cognitive aspects of learning to spell: A reflection of word knowledge*. Newark, DE: International Reading Association.

Invernizzi, M., Abouseid, M., & Gill, T. (1994).Using students' invented spellings as a guide for spelling instruction that emphasizes word study. *The Elementary School Journal, 95*, 155–167.

Invernizzi, M., & Worthy, M. (1989). An orthographic-specific comparison of the spellingerrors of learning disabled and normal children across four grade levels of spelling achievement. *Reading Psychology, 10*, 173–188.

Morris, D. (Ed.). (1989a). *Reading Psychology: An International Quarterly, 10*, 2.

Morris, D. (Ed.). (1989b). *Reading Psychology: An International Quarterly, 10*, 3.

Morris, D. (1993). The relationship between children's concept of word in text and phoneme awareness in learning to read: A longitudinal study. *Research in the Teaching of English, 27*, 133–154.

Morris, D., Blanton, L., Blanton, W.E., Nowacek, J., & Perney, J. (1995). Teaching low-achieving spellers at their "instructional level." *The Elementary School Journal, 96*, 163–178.

Morris, D., Bloodgood, J.W., Lomax, R.G., & Perney, J. (2003). Developmental steps in learning to read: A longitudinal study in kindergarten and first grade. *Reading Research Quarterly, 38*, 302–328.

Morris, D., & Perney, J. (1984). Development spelling as a predictor of first-grade reading achievement. *The Elementary School Journal, 84*, 440–457.

Nagy, W., & Anderson, R. (1984). How many words are there in printed school English? *Reading Research Quarterly, 19*, 303–330.

Nagy, W., & Anderson, R. (1989). Morphological families in the internal lexicon. *Reading Research Quarterly, 24*, 262–282.

Nagy, W., Anderson, R., & Diakidoy, I.A. (1993). The acquisition of morphology: Learning the contribution of suffixes to the meaning of derivatives. *Journal of Reading Behavior, 25*, 155–170.

Nagy, W., Herman, P., & Anderson, R. (1985). Learning words from context. *Reading Research Quarterly, 20*, 233–253.

National Institute of Child Health and Human Development. (2000). *Report of the National Reading Panel. Teaching children to read: An evidence-based assessment of the scientific research literature on reading and its implications for reading instruction* (NIH Publication No. 00-4769). Washington, DC: U.S. Government Printing Office.

Read, C. (1971). Pre-school children's knowledge of English phonology. *Harvard Educational Review, 41*, 1–34.

Read, C. (1975). Children's categorization of speech sounds in English. *Monographs of the National Council of Teachers of English* (No. 17). Urbana, IL: National Council of Teachers of English.

CHAPTER 11

Teacher Education and Professional Development in Reading: 50 Years of Learning

Donna M. Ogle

Donna M. Ogle

As a young university professor working with preservice and master's level teachers and consulting in schools where our graduates were employed, it didn't take me long to notice that many of my best students weren't implementing in the classroom many of the ideas they had learned through their coursework. This realization led me to focus much of my work in schools, as part of situated professional development. I have been part of districtwide curriculum development projects, textbook adoptions, responses to federally mandated integration, and research and instructional reform initiatives. For many years, I consulted with the National Urban Alliance, because I believe U.S. urban schools most need support in literacy. I experienced real cross-cultural engagement with European and Asian teacher educators through the Reading and Writing for Critical Thinking Project of the International Reading Association (IRA). Most recently I have directed two literacy grants in Chicago Public Schools and serve as senior consultant to the Chicago Striving Readers Project. I continue to be challenged by how to make both my teaching and my work in the schools coherent and mutually supportive.

An Essential History of Current Reading Practices, edited by Mary Jo Fresch.
© 2008 by the International Reading Association.

of professional development and concludes by exploring the current emphasis on teacher and school development and instructional reform.

Teacher Preparation: A Lifelong Journey That Begins With Initial Certification

In their initial survey of preservice teacher preparation to teach reading Austin and Morrison concluded that few programs adequately prepared teachers to teach reading. Fifteen years later, their follow-up survey, *The Torch Lighters Revisited* (Morrison & Austin, 1976), indicated that several improvements had been made in undergraduate teacher preparation programs with broader coverage of content, more courses required, and more field-based or clinical experiences. However, they found little indication of any continuing contact with students once they had graduated from their preservice programs.

Teacher Education Reform: The Holmes Group

Over the subsequent years, concerns continued about the quality and nature of preservice teacher education programs. A major call to reform teacher preparation programs came in the mid-1980s. Major research universities under the leadership of Judith Lanier formed the Holmes Group, a consortium initiated by their education deans that focused on improving the quality of teaching and teacher preparation. The report they prepared (The Holmes Group, 1986) included many strong recommendations for increased focus on quality teaching at the universities, as well as in the preparation of teachers. One of the specific recommendations included in the report was to shift teacher preparation to a fifth-year program after completion of undergraduate education. While the creation of this new approach to teacher education at the member universities was general and not focused in reading education, the outcome of their decision to shift teacher preparation totally to the fifth-year master's program with "a successful year of well-supervised internship" (p. 94) has clearly affected the quality and nature of teacher preparation in reading at those schools. Education students focus on other concentrations during their first four years and then must learn all about teaching during a concentrated year. Some states, such as California, have also adopted the same model for teacher education, arguing that teachers need a strong foundation in the liberal arts to teach well. However, the impact of these programs on students' ability to absorb and develop their own understanding of teaching and learning has not been systematically studied.

developed to reflect those competencies. These standards-based guidelines have, in turn, been used in the development of rigorous state teacher testing programs in several states. For example, California requires teaching candidates to pass the Reading Instruction Competency Assessment, the RICA (a full description of the test is available at the RICA website, www.rica.nesinc.com).

IRA has also participated in the development of standards for teacher education programs and serves as the evaluator for NCATE applications for reading programs (see IRA's website, www.reading.org, for further information).

U.S. Federal Initiatives in Reading

Since the turn of the 21st century, there has been a major shift in federal involvement in education. The federal government has also become much more prescriptive in reading education; the National Reading Panel's (NRP) report (National Institute of Child Health and Human Development, 2000) has become a centerpiece in federal initiatives. The congressional funding and requirements included in the No Child Left Behind (NCLB) Act of 2001 and the subsequent development of the Reading First program specify the implementation of assessments, targeted instructional programs, and instructional foci (see also chapters 2, 3, 7, and 9, this volume, for more discussion of NCLB and Reading First). This attempt to determine the content of reading instruction has also included university course content. The National Council on Teacher Quality (NCTQ; Walsh, Glass, & Wilcox, 2006), a U.S. federally supported group, recently reviewed the content of the reading course syllabi from a wide variety of teacher preparation institutions across the country. They used the NRP report's core components of the "science of reading"—phonics, phonemic awareness, fluency, vocabulary and comprehension strategies—as the indicators of the quality of the courses. Included in their evaluation were the textbooks that instructors were using. Both universities and publishers have challenged this review and the subsequent report. However, it clearly represents an assertive and prescriptive approach at the federal level to curriculum and content in reading education.

The U.S. government has also increased requirements for the assessment of reading, requiring that states annually test students and that the National Assessment of Educational Progress (NAEP) in reading be administered in all states every two years. Within the NCLB legislation, Reading First also prescribes how reading is to be taught and stipulates the kinds of professional development teachers receive. The legacy of this administration's activist involvement in education is yet to be known. It clearly is attempting to move reading education in a different direction.

teachers. They knew how to focus and had a perspective about teaching and learning that other new teachers did not. "The differences in prospective teachers' knowledge and beliefs were very clear and the classrooms were also distinguishable from those of various comparison groups. There were also differences in the level of child engagement with texts" (Risko et al., in review, p. 72).

These findings are particularly interesting when compared to the recent report of the NCTQ (Walsh et al., 2006). In this study of required elementary reading education courses, none of the case study schools in the third phase of the IRA study was included. The study only looked at course content and texts used in required early reading courses with no attempt to evaluate the impact of the courses on actual teaching. The conclusion of that study was that few reading education programs are preparing students with the knowledge of the "science of reading," yet the study made no attempt to look at the quality of field experiences or the classroom teaching those students could provide. Nor was there an examination of the range of courses students might take in a given program. What the study did find was that recent research results consistent with National Institute of Child Health and Development were not well represented in the courses students took or in the textbooks they were asked to read.

What emerges is a field with a wide variety of approaches to the preparation of teachers at both the undergraduate and the master's levels. There seems to be a general recognition that there is a great deal to be known before teachers can provide the quality of instruction that is demanded in the increasingly diverse and challenging educational environment. How to prepare teachers within the framework of undergraduate and master's level of education does not have a single or simple answer. Indeed, it seems that there is a growing recognition that preservice work only begins to lay the foundation for subsequent learning while teaching. There is also great diversity in what is considered important for students to know about teaching reading.

Continuing Teacher Preparation: The Role of Ongoing School-Based Professional Development

Most educators and researchers agree that preservice preparation is only the starting point for continued learning once teachers are in schools working with students. The extensive research by Darling-Hammond (1998) demonstrated the importance of focusing efforts on developing quality teachers. She explained, while summarizing Ball and Cohen's work, that learning found in "rich professional development settings" is characterized as

professional development sessions every year or every set number of years. While this form of continued learning provides many options to teachers and helps them determine where their own interests and needs are, it does little to affect their instruction. And the faculties who teach courses at universities are very aware that there is a real disconnect between what graduate students/teachers are able to do for courses and what they will actually implement in their teaching (Anders & Richardson, 1994; Bean, 2004).

One way to bridge "academic" study of learning and teaching has been to encourage teachers to engage teacher researchers, examining in a systematic way aspects of their own teaching. Stimulating teacher reflection and inquiry into their own practices has led to groups of teachers who meet and share their work, sometimes within the school structure, sometimes as independent groups, and sometimes with university encouragement and support. For many teachers, focusing on their own practice has helped them continue to grow. The National Board for Professional Teaching Standards has created another way for teachers to continue to develop deeper reflection on their practice and, at the same time, has provided financial incentives and recognition for teachers who are successful in gaining this advanced certification.

The tension between individual teacher development and the needs of schools is a real one. Some school districts have developed a menu of options for teachers so they could continue their learning in areas of choice. Teacher Centers and/or Professional Development Schools offering short courses taught by local teachers and other consultants are in place in many districts to meet the wide learning needs of their faculties.

Schoolwide Curriculum Development

None of the options described in the previous section directly addresses the needs of school districts for improvement in curriculum and instruction in core learning areas or in models of behavior management and school culture. As teachers grow in their expertise, they should have a leavening impact on the school, but that may or may not occur. Studies of attempts to change instructional practice point to the importance of the school context in determining what teachers will actually use from what they learn (Allington & Cunningham, 2006; Guskey, 1986; Ogle & Hunter, 2001). Therefore, a third traditional form of continuing professional development has been focused on schoolwide curriculum development efforts in which teachers learn together over some period of time. Often these efforts are focused on the implementation of some new curriculum program or program of classroom management

spotlight on professional development and has supported the exploration of ways to make that most effective.

One form of the effort to improve instruction through professional development and schoolwide programs has been the development and spread of several general Comprehensive School Reform (CSR) models (Borman, Hewes, Overman, & Brown, 2003). Each program has a clear focus with varying degrees of research supporting their emphases. Each has a national project team that contracts with schools or districts to provide professional training and support so teachers can develop consistent instructional practices. CSR programs have been popular in many districts because they have a coherent instructional framework across the grades and provide trainers and coaches.

Every Child, Every School: Success for All (Slavin, Madden, Dolan, & Wasik, 1996) and the Oregon Direct Instruction Model (Meyer, 1984) are among the most widely adopted professional development models in reading. The focus on comprehensive school reform models and on the development of classroom-based networks such as Reading Recovery and the Lesley College Literacy Collaborative (information available at www.lesley.edu/crr) have led to more prescriptions regarding the nature of reading instruction provided by teachers in schools in those programs. In some settings, this has been accepted, and teachers have been willing to work toward a more unified focus.

However, recent research reviewing the full range of CSR programs (Borman et al., 2003) indicates a mixed pattern of results with some models showing positive effects, but in 35% of the studies reviewed in their meta-analysis, the control groups showed higher outcomes than the reform models. Borman's analysis also found that the effects of the comprehensive reform models increased substantially after the fifth year. Interestingly, improved results with the models between the fifth and seventh years were correlated with lower staff development support. In analyzing these results, Marzano, Waters, and McNulty (2005) suggested that when close adherence to the models did not produce the kinds of gains promised over time, schools modified them to meet local needs and thus were more able to take advantage of their strengths. They conclude, "Only when schools adapt a CSR model to their specific situation does it positively affect student achievement" (p. 80).

Balancing Teacher Development With School Staff Needs

Districts are often caught between the desire to adopt a model program and the desire to create their own site-specific programs. Taylor and Pearson's (2002) review of effective schools concludes that

implemented in schools. As Anders, Hoffman, and Duffy (2000) noted in their review of both pre- and inservice teacher education, less than 1% of the reading research studies since 1965 have dealt with either area.

In reviewing professional development research, one needs to look to the more general work done in school change and staff development. Our own field has not developed rich models or tested them in research. What generally exists are small-scale studies and reports of specific implementation efforts (Bean, 2004; Bizar & Barr, 2001; Cooter, 2004; Lapp et al., 2004; Ogle & Fogelberg, 2001; Risko & Bromley, 2001). In the introduction to their seminal study of literacy staff development with teachers in grades 3–5, Anders and Richardson (1994) noted, "Many staff development programs may be fragmented and exclude the research and theoretical connections" (p. 6). They also criticized many staff development programs because of their top-down nature as they try to "import specific information to teachers for the purpose of changing their behavior" (p. 8).

Illustrative Studies

In response to these concerns, Anders and Richardson's *The Reading Instruction Study* (1994) was designed to examine the implementation or lack of implementation of current research of reading and literacy and to suggest more effective teaching strategies and more effective methods of training teachers. It was part of an effort funded by the U.S. Department of Education's Office of Educational Research and Instruction (1986–1992). As Anders explained in the opening pages,

> My experience [as a reading specialist responsible for staff development to help content area teachers] led me to believe that telling teachers about exciting and innovative new practices did not necessarily lead to implementation of those practices. I felt there was a clear need to better understand the nature of teachers' beliefs, teachers' practice, and teacher change. (p. 2)

Together, Anders and Richardson applied for a federal research grant on professional development. Subsequently they designed a collaborative, inquiry model that involved them in discussions with teachers about reading instructional practices and in helping individual teachers observe their own instruction through videotaped segments and develop their own "practical argument" about their literacy instruction (Fenstermacher & Richardson, 1993). The actual study involved fourth- to sixth-grade teachers from five different school districts. The researchers concluded that inviting teachers to be partners in exploration of their practices and priorities produced a positive context for both teacher and university faculty growth.

to watch literacy instruction develop over the course of the year. Yet another project, Project READ, is focused on developing leadership teams that define particular standards-based outcomes for their schools and engage in an articulated process of school reform.

These partnerships reflect the realization that, within a large urban district, schools vary tremendously and specific staff development programs can be responsive to these variations. After four years, the evaluation of the projects indicated that student gains in the project schools exceeded those of comparable CPS schools (Hanson, DiSteffano, Blachowicz, Mueller, & Eason-Watkins, 2006). As the work has proceeded, the university teams and the external evaluators have been able to identify school-based factors that differentiate successful schools from those where the partnerships have not been as productive. Key factors emanating from the site visits and interviews, as well as data analysis, have been organized into a framework for improving literacy instruction, which includes the following seven dimensions:

1. Effective literacy leadership
2. High-quality, in-school professional development
3. Exemplary assessment practices
4. Coherent and effective literacy curriculum and instruction
5. Professional literacy communities
6. Learning oriented student literacy achievement, behavior, and attitudes
7. An infrastructure that supports sustainable efforts

These dimensions don't delineate the variety of ways the focus on literacy was cultivated within the development projects themselves. For example, in the first years, the National-Louis University Literacy Partners schools developed a specific reading curriculum framework that included vocabulary/word study, comprehension, fluency, and scaffolded independent reading. Teachers were supported as they implemented guided reading, created literacy centers, collected and leveled books, and modeled reading for their students. Most of these differentiated practices had not been part of teachers' routines, but with university partners working closely with teachers over three years many of these practices began to seem more natural. The last two years have seen a shift to developing confidence and sharing among the teachers so they can be instructional leaders in their buildings and the focus on quality instructional practices can be maintained. From our own experiences in the same five-year Chicago

Considerations for Future Research

With a small proportion of research in literacy being devoted to teacher development, it is clear that a shift in priorities is in order. As the stakes keep going up for teachers in the field, high-quality support structures are definitely needed that help teachers to be most effective as mentors and teachers for a wide range of students. Several issues deserve our attention:

- More study of alternative programs in teacher preparation is clearly required. There is almost no research on the impact of fifth-year programs in preparing quality reading teachers, compared with a more integrated and sustained learning over three to four years in undergraduate coursework. Alternative certification programs and the impact on students of putting untrained young graduates in primary classrooms deserve attention.

- Research is needed to help determine the right balance between knowledge building and practicum experiences and the location of those experiences either in clinical settings or in classrooms.

- We need to develop good models linking preservice with ongoing professional development once teachers are in school classrooms.

- Teachers vary considerably in how they learn and how they teach. More attention is needed on how variations and preferences can be supported while still building schools where there is a shared focus and approach to literacy.

- The cost of teacher preparation is quite high; more attention needs to be given to creating effective university and college education programs with adequate resources to support novice teacher candidates.

- Schools have increasingly diverse student populations. At the same time there are fewer minority teachers. A large issue for the future is creating contexts in which teachers can study, experiment, and develop effective instructional programs for all students. Preparing more minority teachers is also essential.

- Ongoing research is needed on ways for teacher education programs in colleges and universities to collaborate more effectively with public schools in implementing quality instruction.

We have come a long way in the last 50 years. The importance of highly qualified teachers and of providing support for their continued learning have been established in the research and through studies of schools that make a

The key is responding to personal, motivational, and learning variations in students, teachers, and administrators. Schools that are most successful with challenging students have created contexts where teachers feel respected and where they collaborate in solving instructional issues. Currently, the press for achievement and test results may depress individual teacher efforts to think deeply about their own instructional decisions. There must be support for teacher reflection, decision making, and growth. Script readers don't make collaborative coaches and stimulators of students' inquiry and confidence. Teachers need to be encouraged to listen to students, to hypothesize about what they are thinking, and to make sound instructional decisions (Hoffman & Pearson, 2000).

The research on high-poverty schools that have been successful in raising literacy achievement of their students indicates that these schools that "beat the odds" have developed professional supports for teachers so their efforts can be effective. They embody the characteristics of good leadership, nurturing of teachers in a learning community, focus on student growth, and support for all students. Creating such schools is not easy; they are the exceptions, unfortunately. A process-oriented perspective and a clear understanding of the path to school improvement are needed; it is clear that each context has its own promises and challenges, and the answers don't come easily (Au, 2005; Au, Raphael, & Mooney, in press; Cooter, 2004). Yet our commitment needs to be to work together as teams of educators in universities, colleges, centers, and schools so that what we know is translated into rich learning experiences for all students. Creating more of those contexts for the future teachers of the United States, as well as practicing teachers, is our responsibility.

ESSENTIAL READINGS ON TEACHER EDUCATION AND PROFESSIONAL DEVELOPMENT

Carr, J., Herman, N., & Harris, D.E. (2005). *Creating dynamic schools through mentoring, coaching, and collaboration.* Alexandria, VA: Association for Supervision and Curriculum Development.

Costa, A.L., & Garmston, R.J. (1994). *Cognitive coaching: A foundation for Renaissance schools.* Norwood, MA: Christopher-Gordon.

Hoffman, J.V., & Pearson, P.D. (2000). Reading teacher preparation in the next millennium: What your grandmother's teacher didn't know that your granddaughter's teacher should. *Reading Research Quarterly, 35,* 28–44.

Hoffman, J.V., & Pearson, P.D. (2000). Reading teacher preparation in the next millennium: What your grandmother's teacher didn't know that your granddaughter's teacher should. *Reading Research Quarterly, 35,* 28–44.

Hoffman, J.V., Roller, C., Maloch, B., Sailors, M., Duffy, G., & Beretvas, S.N. (2005). Teachers' preparation to teach reading and their experiences and practices in the first three years of teaching. *The Elementary School Journal, 105,* 267–287.

Hoffman, J.V., Roller, C.M., & National Commission on Excellence in Elementary Teacher Preparation for Reading Instruction. (2001). The IRA excellence in reading teacher preparation commission's report: Current practices in reading teacher education at the undergraduate level in the United States. In C.M. Roller (Ed.), *Learning to teach reading: Setting the research agenda* (pp. 32–79). Newark, DE: International Reading Association.

The Holmes Group. (1986). *Tomorrow's teachers: A report of the Holmes Group.* East Lansing, MI: Author.

Hord, S.M., Rutherford, W.L., Huling-Austin, L., & Hall, G.E. (1987). *Taking charge of change.* Alexandria, VA: Association for Supervision and Curriculum Development.

International Reading Association. (1998). *Standards for reading professionals.* Newark, DE: Author.

International Reading Association. (2003). *Prepared to make a difference: The report of the National Commission on Excellence in Elementary Teacher Preparation for Reading Instruction.* Newark, DE: Author.

International Reading Association. (2004). *Standards for reading professionals—Revised 2003.* Newark, DE: Author.

International Reading Association. (2006). *Standards for middle and high school literacy coaches.* Newark, DE: Author.

Jetton, T.L., & Dole, J.A. (Eds.). (2004). *Adolescent literacy research and practice.* New York: Guilford.

Lapp, D., Block, C.C., Copper, E.J., Flood, J., Roser, N., & Tinajero, J.V. (Eds.). (2004). *Teaching all the children: Strategies for developing literacy in an urban setting.* New York: Guilford.

Loucks-Horsley, S., Harding, C.K., Arbuckle, M.A., Murray, L.B., Dubea, C., & Williams, M. (1987). *Continuing to learn: A guidebook for teacher development.* Oxford, OH: National Staff Development Council.

Maryland State Task Force on Reading. (2002). Retrieved November 10, 2006, from www.ecs.org/dbsearches/Search_Info/Literacy_Program Profile.asp?ProgID=126

Marzano, R.J., Waters, T., & McNulty, B.A. (2005). *School leadership that works: From research to results.* Alexandria, VA: Association for Supervision and Curriculum Development.

Meyer, L.A. (1984). Long-term academic effects of the Direct Instruction project follow through. *The Elementary School Journal, 84,* 380–394.

Morrison, C., & Austin, M.C. (1976). The torch lighters revisited. A preliminary report. *The Reading Teacher, 29,* 647–652.

National Institute of Child Health and Human Development. (2000). *Report of the National Reading Panel. Teaching children to read: An evidence-based assessment of the scientific research literature on reading and its implications for reading instruction* (NIH Publication No. 00-4769). Washington, DC: U.S. Government Printing Office.

Ogle, D. (2003). Meeting the challenges for all students in urban schools. In D. Lapp, C.C. Block, E.J. Cooper, J. Flood, N. Roser, & J.V. Tinajero (Eds.), *Teaching all the children: Strategies for developing literacy in an urban setting* (pp. 327–335). New York: Guilford.

Ogle, D. (2005). The seduction of simple solutions: A response to Doug Reeves. In J. Flood & P. Anders (Eds.), *Literacy development of students in urban schools* (pp. 389–397). Newark, DE: International Reading Association.

Ogle, D., & Fogelberg, E. (2001). Expanding collaborative roles of reading specialists: Developing an intermediate reading support team. In V.J. Risko & K. Bromley (Eds.), *Collaboration for diverse learners: Viewpoints and practices* (pp. 152–167). Newark, DE: International Reading Association.

Ogle, D., & Hunter, K. (2001). Case study of school change. In M. Bizar & R. Barr (Eds.), *School change in a time of urban reform* (pp. 179–194). Mahwah, NJ: Erlbaum.

Richardson, V., & Anders, P. (1994). The study of teacher change. In V. Richardson (Ed.), *Teacher change and the staff development process: A case in reading instruction* (pp. 159–180). New York: Teachers College Press.

Risko, V., & Bromley, K. (Eds.). (2001). *Collaboration for diverse learners: Viewpoints and practices.* Newark, DE: International Reading Association.

Risko, V., Roller, C., Cummins, C., Bean, R., Block, C.C., Anders, P., et al. (in review). *A critical review of the research on teacher preparation for reading instruction.*

AUTHOR INDEX

INVERNIZZI, M., 46, 192, 195–196, 203
IRWIN, J.W., 101

J

JANSKY, J.J., 170
JEHNG, J.C., 20
JENKINS, J., 197
JETTON, T.L., 17, 19–20, 76, 130–131, 218
JETT-SIMPSON, M., 76
JOHNSON, D.D., 88
JOHNSON, E., 126
JOHNSON, S., 187
JOHNSTON, F., 46, 195–196
JONES, W., 76
JUDY, J.E., 18, 131
JUEL, C., 49, 174, 176
JUNGEBLUT, A., 126

K

KAME'ENUI, E.J., 93–94, 198, 203
KAMIL, M.L., 17, 27, 101, 214, 226
KATZ, L., 22
KAVANAGH, J.F., 38
KEENAN, D.M., 126
KELLY, A.E., 131
KELLY, M., 130
KEOGH, B.K., 16
KEPHART, N.C., 166
KETT, J.F., 126
KING, J.R., 18
KINTSCH, W., 18, 88, 99
KINZER, C.K., 98, 135
KIRK, S.A., 166
KIRSCH, I.S., 126
KIST, W., 135
KLESIUS, J.P., 176
KLIEBARD, H.M., 3
KLINGNER, J.K., 18
KLOTZ, J., 132
KNAPP, M.S., 49
KNIGHT, S.L., 26
KONOPAK, B.C., 18
KONOPAK, J.P., 18
KOZEN, A.A., 133
KRAMER, K., 135
KUCAN, L., 200, 202
KUHN, M.R., 113–117
KULIKOWICH, J.M., 131

L

LABBO, L., 135
LABERGE, D., 85, 106, 111
LABOV, W., 16
LANGER, J., 127

LAMOREAUX, L.A., 163
LANGFORD, W.S., 170
LAPP, D., 219
LARRICK, N., 151
LARSEN, S.C., 173
LARSEN, Y.W., 127
LAST, D., 131
LAUER, K.D., 134
LAVE, J., 19
LAYZER, J.I., 54
LEE, D.M.P., 163
LEE, J.J., 94
LEE, W., 61
LEHR, S., 149
LEMS, K., 117
L'ENGLE, M., 145
LENHART, L.A., 111
LESLIE, L., 76
LESTER, J.H., 131, 146
LEU, D.J., JR., 98, 135
LEVIN, H., 15, 39, 111
LEVINE, J.M., 20
LEWIS, J.P., 87
LINEK, W.M., 53
LINN, R.L., 148
LIPSON, M.Y., 19, 91
LOMAX, R.G., 193, 203
LOUCKS-HORSLEY, S., 214
LOVE, A.M., 132
LOVE, K., 135
LUKE, A., 97
LUNDEBERG, M., 18
LYONS, C.A., 226
LYONS, T.T., 13
LYSYNCHUK, L.M., 18

M

MACAULAY, D., 146
MADDEN, N.A., 217
MALOCH, B., 208, 210
MANDL, H., 18
MARCUS, L.S., 154
MARTIN, B., JR, 146
MARTINEZ, M.G., 116, 147, 153–154
MARYLAND STATE TASK FORCE ON READING, 210
MARZANO, R.J., 217
MASLAND, R.L., 173
MASLOW, A.H., 121
MASON, J.A., 174
MASTERSON, J., 200
MATHEWSON, G.C., 99
MATHISON, C., 128
MATTHEWS, M.M., 137
MAXWELL, C.M., 55

PEARSON, P.D., 14, 17–18, 27, 38, 41, 43–44, 73, 85–93, 95–97, 99–101, 216–217, 220, 222, 225
PELLEGRINI, A.D., 59
PELOSI, P.L., 183
PEREGOY, S.F., 74, 132
PERFETTI, C., 197–198
PERKINS, D.N., 19
PERNEY, J., 193, 195, 203
PERRET, J., 20
PERRET-CLAREMONT, A., 20
PETERSEN, D.K., 176
PETERSON, B., 151
PETERSON, R., 149
PEYTON, T., 60
PHELPS, S.F., 131
PICK, A., 39
PIKULSKI, J.J., 113
PINNELL, G.S., 67, 70, 72, 74, 77, 79, 113, 151, 226
PLUCK, M., 114
POUNDSTONE, C.C., 21, 130
PRAWAT, R.S., 19
PRESSLEY, M., 18, 76, 83, 93–96, 101, 132, 218
PRITCHARD, R., 132
PROUST, M., 25
PUGH, K.R., 22
PURCELL-GATES, V., 55, 63
PUROHIT, K., 135
PURVES, A.C., 149
PUTNAM, L.R., 3

Q
QUINN, D.W., 114
QUIOCHO, A., 131

R
RANDALL, S., 20
RAND READING STUDY GROUP, 21
RAPHAEL, T.E., 18, 73, 76, 91–92, 96, 133–134, 151, 222, 225
RASINSKI, T.V., 53, 62–63, 95, 109–110, 114–117, 193
READ, C., 112, 189, 203
READENCE, J.E., 18, 121, 125, 134, 138
REDER, L.M., 19
REED, J.H., 21
REESE, D., 68–69
REINKING, D., 92, 130, 135
RESNICK, L.B., 20
REUTZEL, D.R., 74, 110
REYNOLDS, R.E., 17–19, 131
RICCIUTI, A., 61

RICE, M.E., 21
RICHARDSON, J.S., 121, 129, 131, 134–135
RICHARDSON, V., 215, 219–220
RICHGELS, D., 190
RICKELMAN, R.J., 121, 138
RIDGEWAY, V.G., 130
RIPPERE, V., 149
RISKO, V., 213, 219
RISLEY, T.R., 57–58, 200, 203
RO, J.M., 147, 181
ROBERTS, L., 129
ROBINSON, F.P., 123
ROBINSON, H.A., 121, 123, 125, 138
ROBINSON, H.M., 84
ROBINSON, R.D., 132
ROEHLER, L.R., 18, 91, 93
ROGOFF, B., 19
ROHRER, J.H., 109
ROLLER, C.M., 208, 210, 212, 213
ROSEN, M.J., 171
ROSENBLATT, L.M., 19, 23, 89, 99, 144, 148
ROSER, N., 116, 219
ROUTMAN, R., 71, 74, 79
ROWLING, J.K., 146
RUBIN, R., 171
RUDDELL, R.B., 14, 38, 92, 99, 101, 178
RUDOLPH, M., 36
RUDORPH, E., 188
RUMELHART, D.E., 18, 88, 99, 131
RUTHERFORD, W.L., 216
RYCIK, J.A., 123, 132

S
SADOSKI, M., 88, 99
SAILORS, M., 208, 210
SALOMON, G., 20
SAMUELS, S.J., 17, 83, 85, 99, 106, 110–112, 116, 118
SANDERS, P., 125
SAPHIER, J.D., 173
SAPIN, C., 54, 61, 63
SAUL, E.W., 14
SCANLON, D., 130
SCARBOROUGH, H.S., 148
SCARDAMALIA, M., 20
SCHALLERT, D.L., 18–19, 21
SCHARER, P., 191–192
SCHATSCHNEIDER, C., 21–22
SCHATZ, E., 199
SCHEFFLER, A.J., 135
SCHLAGAL, R., 195
SCHMITT, C., 160
SCHREIBER, P.A., 107, 112, 116, 118
SCHUDER, T., 93–94

CONDITIONED LEARNING: era of, 13–15

CONSTRUCTIVISM, 19–20, 43–45; and content area reading, 133; and spelling, 188

CONTENT AREA READING: definition of, 122; early influences on, 122–123; essential readings on, 137–138; future of, 136–137; history of, 120–143

CONTEXT: expanding notion of, 97; and vocabulary, 198–199

CONTINUING TEACHER EDUCATION, 213–214

CRITICAL LITERACY, 95

CSR. *See* Comprehensive School Reform

CUEING SYSTEMS, 42–43, 111

CULLINAN, BERNICE, 151

CURRICULUM DEVELOPMENT: schoolwide, 215–217

D

DECODING INSTRUCTION, 39; and fluency, 115

DELIGHT: guided reading and, 76–77

DERIVATIONAL CONSTANCY STAGE: of word knowledge, 191

DIAGNOSTIC/PRESCRIPTIVE TEACHING, 171–173

DIRECTED READING ACTIVITY, 68, 69*t*

DISCUSSION: and comprehension, 94

DISTAR READING, 41

DIVERSITY: and children's literature, 151; and content area reading, 134

E

EARLY ALPHABETIC STAGE: of word knowledge, 191

EDUCATION FOR ALL HANDICAPPED CHILDREN ACT, 173

EFFERENT STANCE, 89

ELEMENTARY AND SECONDARY EDUCATION ACT (ESEA), 150, 170

ELKONIN BOXES, 43

ELOQUENT ORAL READING, 108

EMERGENT LITERACY: term, 87

EMOTIONAL DISTURBANCE: and reading delays, 160, 163

ENGAGED LEARNING: and comprehension, 92–94; era of, 20–22

ENGLISH AS A SECOND LANGUAGE (ESL): and content area reading, 132, 134

ESEA. *See* Elementary and Secondary Education Act

ESSENTIAL READINGS: on children's literature, 154; on comprehension, 100–101; on content area reading, 137–138; on family literacy, 63; on fluency, 117–118; on guided reading, 79; on history of reading, 26–27; on phonics instruction, 49; on remedial reading, 182–183; on spelling and vocabulary, 203; on teacher education and professional development, 225–226

EVEN START, 60–61

EXPERTS: characteristics of, 5–6

F

FAMILY LITERACY: definition of, 54–55; essential readings on, 63; future of, 62; history of, 52–65; pivotal studies in, 55–59; political influences on, 59–61

FEDERAL GOVERNMENT: and teacher education, 211. *See also* No Child Left Behind Act

FIRST GRADE STUDIES, 15, 38

FLUENCY: current status of, 113–116; early conceptions of, 108–109; essential readings on, 117–118; future of, 116–117; history of, 106–119; recommendations for, 114

FORD, MICHAEL P., 66–81

FOUR BLOCKS LITERACY MODEL, 45–46

FOX, EMILY, 12–32

FRESCH, MARY JO, 1–11

LITERACY LEAD TEACHERS, 222
LOOK-SAY METHOD: Flesch on, 14

M

MATTHEW EFFECTS, 178, 198
McCORMICK, SANDRA, 157–185
McLAUGHLIN, MAUREEN, 82–105
MEANING: reading for, guided reading and, 75
MEDICAL MODEL: of reading instruction, 14
MEMORY PROCESSES: defective, 171
METACOGNITION: and comprehension, 91; guided reading and, 76
MISCUE, 173, 188; term, 86
MIXED DOMINANCE, 160
MODEL: definition of, 128
MOTIVATION, 21
MRAZ, MARYANN, 106–119
MULTIPLE CAUSATION, 171

N

NATIONAL ASSESSMENT OF EDUCATIONAL PROGRESS (NAEP), 211
NATIONAL BOARD FOR PROFESSIONAL TEACHING STANDARDS, 215
NATIONAL COUNCIL ON TEACHER QUALITY (NCTQ), 211, 213
NATIONAL-LOUIS UNIVERSITY LITERACY PARTNERS, 221
NATIONAL READING PANEL (NRP), 115–116; and remedial reading, 180–181
NATIONAL RIGHT-TO-READ PROGRAM, 173
NATURAL LEARNING: era of, 15–17
NEUROBIOLOGICAL APPROACH: to reading, 95
NEUROLOGICAL IMPRESS METHOD, 112
NEW LITERACIES: and children's literature, 152; comprehension and, 98–99; and content area reading, 131, 135
NO CHILD LEFT BEHIND ACT: and content area reading, 133; and family literacy, 60; and phonics instruction, 47; and remedial reading, 180–181; and teacher education, 211, 216
NONFICTION TEXTS, 146
NRP. *See* National Reading Panel

O

OGLE, DONNA M., 207–228
ONSETS, 46
OPITZ, MICHAEL F., 66–81
ORAL LANGUAGE INSTRUCTION: and phonics, 34–35
ORAL READING: and fluency, 108
ORAL READING ERROR: term, 86
OREGON DIRECT INSTRUCTION MODEL, 217
ORTON-GILLINGHAM APPROACH, 170

P

PADAK, NANCY, 52–65
PARENTAL INVOLVEMENT. *See* family literacy
PERINATAL CAUSES, 171
PHONEMIC AWARENESS, 44–45
PHONETIC STAGE: of word knowledge, 191

S

SCAFFOLDING, 42; in guided reading, 74

SCHEMA THEORY, 18; and comprehension, 83, 88, 90–91; and content area reading, 131–132

SEMANTIC CUES, 42–43

SEMIPHONETIC STAGE: of word knowledge, 191

SES. *See* socioeconomic status

SILENT READING, 70, 70*t*; and fluency, 109

SKEPTICISM, 24–25

SKILLS MOVEMENT, 37, 39–41

SMALL-GROUP INSTRUCTION, 71–74. *See also* guided reading

SOCIOCULTURAL LEARNING: and comprehension, 90, 94; era of, 19–20

SOCIOECONOMIC STATUS (SES): and reading development, 57–58, 58*t*

SOCIOLINGUISTS, 16

SOUND–SYMBOL RELATIONSHIPS, 39–40

SPELLING, 186–206; delay in, 192; essential readings on, 203; future of, 200–201; phonics instruction and, 45–46; and reading, 193–194

SQ3R STRATEGY, 123

SRR, 123

STAGE THEORY: of word knowledge, 191–192

STANCE, 89

STANDARDS-BASED LEARNING: and content area reading, 133–135; and remedial reading, 180–181; and teacher education, 210–211

STORY GRAMMAR, 88, 91

STRATEGY: versus activity, 128, 130

STRATEGY INSTRUCTION, 18, 44; and comprehension, 91, 93–95; and content area reading, 127, 129–132

STUDY SKILLS, 135

SUBSTRATA THEORY: of reading, 37

SYLLABLE JUNCTURE STAGE: of word knowledge, 191

SYNTACTIC CUES, 43

SYNTAX PERRSPECTIVE, 37

SYNTHETIC PHONICS, 37, 40

T

TEACHER EDUCATION: continuing, 213–214; essential readings on, 225–226; future research directions for, 223–224; history of, 207–228; need for research on, 218–222; and school change, 214–218

TEACHER EXPECTATIONS FOR STUDENT ACHIEVEMENT (TESA), 216

TEXT: changing nature of, 97

TITLE I, 59

TRANSACTION: with literature, 148–149; term, 89

TRANSACTIONAL STRATEGIES INSTRUCTION (TSI), 93

TRANSITIONAL STAGE: of word knowledge, 191

TWO-GENERATION PROGRAMS. *See* family literacy

U–V

UNIVERSITY–SCHOOL PARTNERSHIPS, 220–222

VIRGINIA SCHOOL, 191

VOCABULARY, 186–206; and comprehension, 94; and copmrehension, 93; essential readings on, 203; future of, 201–202; nature of, 196–197; word gap, 57–58, 58*t*, 199–200